A NEW DIRECTION

A Cognitive-Behavioral Treatment Curriculum

LONG-TERM WORKBOOK

Drug & Alcohol Education

Mapping a Life of Recovery & Freedom for Chemically Dependent Criminal Offenders

A Collaboration of Chemical Dependency Professionals from the Minnesota Department of Corrections and the Hazelden Foundation

HAZELDEN®

Hazelden
Center City, Minnesota 55012-0176

1-800-328-9000
1-651-213-4590 (Fax)
www.hazelden.org

ISBN: 1-56838-845-4

Cover design by David Spohn
Interior design by Terri Kinne
Illustrations by Patrice Barton

The book *Free at Last: Daily Meditations by and for Inmates,*
from which quotations appear in this text, is published
and copyrighted by Hazelden Foundation.

Hazelden Publishing and Educational Services is a division of the Hazelden Foundation, a not-for-profit organization. Since 1949, Hazelden has been a leader in promoting the dignity and treatment of people afflicted with the disease of chemical dependency.

The mission of the foundation is to improve the quality of life for individuals, families, and communities by providing a national continuum of information, education, and recovery services that are widely accessible; to advance the field through research and training; and to improve our quality and effectiveness through continuous improvement and innovation.

Stemming from that, the mission of this division is to provide quality information and support to people wherever they may be in their personal journey—from education and early intervention, through treatment and recovery, to personal and spiritual growth.

The headquarters of the Hazelden Foundation are in Center City, Minnesota. Additional treatment facilities are located in Chicago, Illinois; New York, New York; Plymouth, Minnesota; St. Paul, Minnesota; and West Palm Beach, Florida. At these sites, we provide a continuum of care for men and women of all ages. Our Plymouth facility is designed specifically for youth and families.

For more information on Hazelden, please call **1-800-257-7800.** Or you may access our World Wide Web site on the Internet at **www.hazelden.org.**

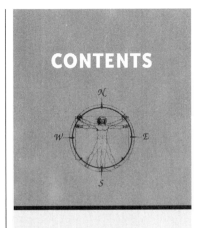

CONTENTS

A NEW DIRECTION

A Cognitive-Behavioral Treatment Curriculum

Acknowledgments

Thanks to all who have contributed to this curriculum:

Sheryl Ramstad Hvass
Commissioner, Minnesota Department of Corrections

Peter Bell
Executive Vice President, Hazelden Publishing and Educational Services

James D. Kaul, Ph.D.
Director, TRIAD Chemical Dependency Program
Minnesota Department of Corrections

Will Alexander
Sex Offender/Chemical Dependency Services Unit, Minnesota Department of Corrections

Minnesota Department of Corrections

Sex Offender Treatment Program at Lino Lakes Minnesota Correctional Facility

Robin Goldman, Director
Jim Berg, Program Supervisor
Brian Heinsohn, Corrections Program Therapist
Greg Kraft, Corrections Program Therapist
K. Kaprice Borowski Krebsbach, Corrections Program Therapist
Kevin Nelson, Corrections Program Therapist
Tim Schrupp, Corrections Program Therapist
Pamela Stanchfield, Corrections Program Therapist
Jason Terwey, Corrections Program Therapist
John Vieno, Corrections Program Therapist
Cynthia Woodward, Corrections Program Therapist

TRIAD Chemical Dependency Program at Lino Lakes Minnesota Correctional Facility

Launie Zaffke, Supervisor
Randy Tenge, Supervisor
Carmen Ihlenfeldt, Acting Supervisor
Thomas A. Berner, Corrections Program Therapist
Toni Brezina, Corrections Program Therapist
Jeanie Cooke, Corrections Program Therapist
Ronald J. DeGidio, Corrections Program Therapist
Susan DeGidio, Corrections Program Therapist
Maryann Edgerley, Corrections Program Therapist
Connie Garritsen, Corrections Program Therapist
Gerald Gibcke, Corrections Program Therapist
Anthony Hoheisel, Corrections Program Therapist
Deidra Jones, Corrections Program Therapist
Beth Matchey, Corrections Program Therapist
Jack McGee, Corrections Program Therapist
Jackie Michaelson, Corrections Program Therapist

Hal Palmer, Corrections Program Therapist
Terrance Peach, Corrections Program Therapist
Holly Petersen, Corrections Program Therapist
Linda Rose, Corrections Program Therapist
Kathy Thompson, Corrections Program Therapist
Beverly Welo, Corrections Program Therapist

Reshape Chemical Dependency Program at Saint Cloud Minnesota Correctional Facility

Robert L. Jungbauer, Director
Christine Fortson, Corrections Program Therapist
Tracanne Nelson, Corrections Program Therapist
Jeffrey D. Spies, Corrections Program Therapist

Atlantis Chemical Dependency Program at Stillwater Minnesota Correctional Facility

Bob Reed, Director
Dennis Abitz, Corrections Program Therapist
Bill Burgin, Corrections Program Therapist
Tom Shipp, Corrections Program Therapist

New Dimensions Chemical Dependency Program at Faribault Minnesota Correctional Facility

Michael Coleman, Supervisor
Michele Caron, Corrections Program Therapist

Central Office

Jim Linehan, Corrections Program Therapist

Minnesota Department of Corrections Supervising Agents

Russ Stricker, Correctional Unit Supervisor
Bobbi Chevaliar-Jones, Intensive Supervised Release Agent
William Hafner, Corrections Agent
Gregory Fletcher, 180 Degrees Halfway House

In Addition:

Writers: Corrine Casanova, Deborah Johnson, Stephen Lehman, Joseph M. Moriarity, Paul Schersten.
Designer: Terri Kinne. **Typesetters:** Terri Kinne, Julie Szamocki. **Illustrator:** Patrice Barton.
Prepress: Don Freeman, Kathryn Kjorlien, Rachelle Kuehl, Joan Seim, Tracy Snyder, David Spohn.
Editor: Corrine Casanova. **Copy editors:** Monica Dwyer Abress, Kristal Leebrick, Caryn Pernu.
Proofreaders: Catherine Broberg, Kristal Leebrick. **Marketer:** Michelle Samlaska. **Video production manager:** Alexis Scott.

Special thanks: Any Color Painting Company; Blue Moon Production Company; Eden Re-entry Services; inmates and staff of Lino Lakes, Rush City, and Stillwater Minnesota Correctional Facilities.

Special thanks to Hazelden: Nancy Alliegro, Derrick Crim, Joe Fittipaldi, Carole Kilpela, Nick Motu, Karin Nord, Patricia Owen, Rebecca Post, Teri Ryan, Ann Standing, Sue Thill, and Kris VanHoof-Haines.

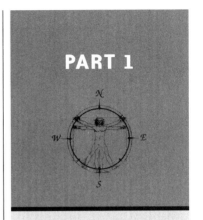

PART 1

A NEW DIRECTION

A Cognitive-Behavioral Treatment Curriculum

Addicts and Addiction

All addicts get to a point where they know something is wrong—that their lives are messed up. They suddenly see just how bad things are. Look at your life. You've lost a lot of things that really matter. Money, relationships, self-respect—even your freedom—have been lost. You're incarcerated now.

Miguel's Story

I am a twenty-one-year-old male who is incarcerated for first-degree aggravated robbery. I've been on my own since I was thirteen. My mom disowned me because I started being really rebellious. At the same time, my father had just gotten incarcerated for attempted murder. Basically, I've raised myself.

I've been around drugs all my life. The first time I drank, and got drunk, I was about ten. It was at a party my parents and their friends were having at our house. One of my uncles gave me a beer. He told me I was old enough now to drink. I drank the beer, but didn't really like the taste. I got a weird feeling from it. After this, my friends and I started stealing beers out of our fridge. I kept on drinking and started smoking weed. I started hanging out more on the streets and then selling for a dealer in return for free drugs. That's how I started smoking crack.

I was always in trouble in school for cutting classes, fighting, and using drugs. I finally got kicked out at fifteen when I started dealing in school. But I didn't really care about that anyway. My home life was a mess. Even when I was younger, my father wasn't around much, and when he was, he was drunk. He'd beat my mom all the time, and me, too. I never knew what was going to set him off. My mother did the same to me when she was high, until I got big enough to defend myself. When my father was around, they would fight and so I would just get high so I wouldn't notice the screaming and hitting. I liked the streets—I was comfortable there. I saw my father selling drugs and carrying guns. My father, my sister, my mother, my relatives—everybody was selling drugs and doing criminal things. I never looked at it as being a negative thing. The only thing I saw was the money. As time went by, I used more and more drugs. I was dealing all the time and then getting high with my homies. There were a few times when I thought maybe I was using too much. I actually tried to stop at this point.

I'd always told myself I could stop anytime I wanted, I just didn't want to. Sometimes, I stopped for a few days at a time but always went back to using. My homies would dis me for stopping. Besides, that's just what we did when we were together. We'd get high and do shit.

My older sister was doing the same things. She finally went to prison for dealing. She and her baby were in prison. She was pregnant when she got sent up and had the baby in prison. Finally, I got caught enough that I did some serious time. For me, it took getting incarcerated with my father to realize that I needed to make a change with myself.

My struggle with addiction has been bad. My negative ideas about treatment were a barrier against me getting the help I needed. At that time, I didn't know how to ask for help without sounding or looking weak and vulnerable to the other prisoners. I believed what I heard that treatment during incarceration was all about "snitching" and "playing the game," that the counselors were "out to get us" and treat us like shit, that I had to uphold the "convict code." Those beliefs were hard to change because up till then my prison time was about upholding the convict code, though I knew better.

I was full of distortions for the first three or four months. I was mainly trying to justify my behavior up to that point in my life. I wanted to leave the program. Without the help from my counselor, I would have bailed from or sabotaged my program long before turning the corner to recovery. I realized that if I didn't change, I would spend the rest of my life in jail on the installment plan just like the other older guys who had been in the program, or I would be killed on the streets, probably by drugs.

— Miguel, incarcerated
A New Direction program participant

The Addiction Tornado

Addiction is like a tornado. It tears through your life and the lives of people you know. It destroys everything it touches. Think about this. If you saw a tornado coming toward you, what would you do? Run for your life, right?

The trouble with addiction is that you don't see it coming until it's too late. Now, you're caught up in it. You're caught up in that addiction tornado. Your life is spinning around in a cycle of drinking or using, crime, and now incarceration.

But you still have a chance to escape. Addiction hasn't killed you yet. If you were running to get out of a tornado, you'd look for a solid building to escape into. This treatment program is like a tornado shelter. It lets you escape the power of addiction until you can get your life together.

If you are reading this, you probably have a problem with alcohol and other drugs—even if you don't think you do. This doesn't mean you are bad, stupid, or weak. There's hope for you to have a better life.

You can be free of addiction. But doing this takes courage and work. Millions of people just like you have beaten their addiction, been released from incarceration, and put their lives together. You can, too.

Insanity is doing the same thing over and over and expecting different results.

If you are like other people who are addicted to alcohol and other drugs, you might be saying some of these things to yourself (this is what we call *self-talk*):

- I don't need help. I can do this myself.
- You people are crazy.
- Nobody cares anyway.
- You're playing with my head.
- I had a tough childhood, so what do people expect?
- I don't use that much.
- I am too screwed up to change.
- I will be okay if I just use less.
- I have to use because of my parents, girlfriend, PO, or _____ (fill in the blank).
- *My* situation is different.
- I can quit anytime. I just don't want to yet.

If you've said any of these things to yourself, you're thinking like an addict. Most addicts have such thoughts at this stage. It's called *denial*. You deny that you have a problem. You make excuses and blame others for your behavior.

An alcoholic walks into a bar and asks the bartender, "Did I spend $200 in here last night?" The bartender says, "Yes." "Thank heavens," says the alcoholic. "I thought I'd lost it."

The addict self-talk in your head can supply countless excuses for not doing anything about your problems with alcohol and other drugs. Here are some examples of that warped thinking:

Myths about Using and Quitting Alcohol and Other Drugs, and Criminal Behavior

- Just this once, and I won't use again.
- I was an alcoholic (crack head, junkie, meth addict, whatever), so weed (or whatever) won't hurt me.
- I've been down a long time.
- I can use; I won't have a UA for at least two weeks.
- Once I get out, everything will be fine.
- You're a real addict only if you use needles.
- I'll just sell, but I won't use.
- I don't have to change my lifestyle. I can just stop drinking or using. I can still have the same friends.
- It's my life, I'll do what I want.
- Marijuana is not a drug because it's not addictive.
- My crime has nothing to do with my addiction.
- I'll just use less next time and I won't get caught.
- I just caught a bad break.
- I can kick this on my own.
- I've been sober during incarceration, so I'll be sober when I get out.
- Addiction is a disease. I can't help myself.
- My drinking or using had nothing to do with my crime.
- I didn't force anyone to buy the drugs.
- I'm just a drug user, not an addict.
- I need to sell to support my family and lifestyle.
- I don't hurt anyone when I use.
- I can't trust anyone.

- I learned my lesson this time.
- I've found religion now. My woman is religious, too, so I won't use.
- Therapists are just using us to get rich. They make money off my being in treatment.
- I don't like the therapist, the group, the program, the people here, talking about myself, or _____ (fill in the blank).
- No one will understand what I do (or did).

It's *now* time to be clear about what is going on with you. If you don't become honest, the addiction tornado will soon catch up to you again.

Let's look at exactly what addiction is and what alcohol and other drugs do to your mind and body.

Remember, delusion is the deadliest part of this illness. That tornado can kill. Get out of the storm. Get into the "treatment" shelter. Accept help.

What Is an Addict? What Is Addiction?

Just what is an addict? This Alcoholics Anonymous story should give you an idea:

> A social drinker, a problem drinker, and an alcoholic walk into a bar. They're all friends. They each order a beer. The bartender brings the beers over. They all have a nice golden color with foamy heads. Almost at the same time, a fly lands on the head of each one of the beers. The social drinker looks at the fly and pushes the beer away. The problem drinker looks at the fly, kind of inches his way over there and flicks the fly off the foam, and drinks his beer. The alcoholic slowly inches his way in there, grabs the fly, and says, "Spit it out, spit it out."

"Some cause happiness wherever they go; others, whenever they go."

— Oscar Wilde

The harder it is to give something up, the more you know you should.

Maybe you've heard that addiction is a disease just like heart problems or diabetes. But you didn't believe it. You said to yourself, "This isn't a disease. I'm *choosing* to use. And if I want, I can choose to stop. I just don't want to stop right now—there's no reason to stop."

Does that sound familiar? Have you said that to yourself or to others? If so, here's another story to think about:

> *Put a cucumber in a jar of vinegar, leave it there a little while, and then take it out—it's still a cucumber. It hasn't turned into a pickle yet. But if you put that cucumber into the jar and leave it there long enough, when you take it out, it will be a pickle. It's hard to say exactly when it turned into a pickle, but you sure can tell when it's not just a cucumber anymore. And most important, once it's pickled, it can never go back to being a cucumber.*

Do you see the point? Social drinkers can drink and use a little and then quit. They're not addicts. But you're different. You keep drinking or using. At some point in time you crossed the line. No matter what you say about being able to stop whenever you want, you haven't. You've changed.

You can't ever go back to how you were before you started drinking and using drugs. You're an addict. Once you're a pickle, you'll never be a cucumber again.

What Exactly Is Addiction?

For many years, people thought that addiction was a sign of poor morals, bad character, and weak willpower. If you were addicted to alcohol or some other drug, you were just a bad person. Fortunately, today we know that's simply not true.

Addiction is a disease. People who become addicted to alcohol or other drugs have bodies that react differently to alcohol and chemicals than the bodies of nonaddicts. As you begin to rescue your life from drugs, it's important to understand what addiction is and what effects drugs have on your body.

Right now, you probably don't see the physical effects of your alcohol and drug use. Addiction is one of the few diseases in which people begin to get better before they realize how sick they were. Your alcohol and drug use hides your illness and the consequences of your behavior from you.

Here are the three main parts of the disease of addiction:

- preoccupation
- loss of control
- relapse

Preoccupation

When people who are addicted spend a lot of time—sometimes even all their time—thinking about, using, and recovering from the effects of their alcohol and drug use, they are said to be preoccupied with drugs or alcohol. This ***preoccupation*** gets in the way of other activities in their lives.

Preoccupation

Preoccupation means thinking and worrying about something a lot. Every day. Even when addicts are doing other things, they are thinking about drugs or alcohol.

An addict is a person who is

1. drinking or using
2. thinking about drinking or using
3. getting over drinking or using

If you know people who are addicted (to whatever drug—meth, crack, alcohol, heroin, for example), you have seen preoccupation. Their whole life is focused on their drug. How to get money to buy it. Where to buy it. Who has the best stuff for the best price. Where to use. How to avoid getting ripped off by some other addict.

Do they think about friends, family, parents, a job, or school? No. Do they even spend time with people who aren't drinking or using? No. Getting the drug and getting high are all they think about. That's preoccupation. More examples include disguising drinking or drug use, hiding alcohol and drugs, and lying about or making excuses for alcohol or drug use.

EXERCISE **1** EXERCISE

Preoccupation with Drinking or Using

➤ How have you been preoccupied with your alcohol and other drug use? Think back to a typical day when you were drinking or using. Follow yourself through that whole day, beginning when you first got up until you went to bed. In the space below, describe all the activities you did that related to your drug use.

_____

_____

_____

_____

_____

_____

_____

_____

_____

Loss of Control

Loss of control doesn't happen every time you use. This is one of the great curses of addiction. It fools you and the people around you once in a while. You believe that if you can manage your use some of the time, then you're not addicted.

Loss of control means that you keep using alcohol or other drugs despite harmful results. These results can be

- legal (being incarcerated because of a drug charge, for example)

- medical (becoming HIV-positive because of injecting drugs)

- family related (getting kicked out of the house because of your alcohol or other drug use)

- financial (being broke and jobless because of your use)

Addicts try switching drugs, cutting down on use, or quitting. But, in the end, addicts can't control their use. Loss of control works together with denial. As your addiction gets worse, you make more excuses for your behavior.

As your addiction gets worse, you make more excuses for your behavior.

Losing Control

Think about a time when you were drinking or using and things got out of control.

➤ What was the situation?

_____

_____

_____

➤ Where were you and who were you with?

_____

_____

_____

➤ What happened that was out of control?

_____

_____

_____

_____

Relapse

The last stage of addiction is relapse. To *relapse* means to begin using drugs or alcohol again after some time of not using.

Just because we say it's a stage of addiction doesn't mean it's okay to relapse. We *are* saying that without help and treatment, you can't quit. Addicts who try to quit on their own (who *don't* complete treatment) *might* be able to stop their drug use *for a while.* But all of them return to drug use. You can't quit on your own. Think about Miguel in this workbook. He stopped drinking or using several times on his own. Without treatment and help from others, he started drinking and using and criminal activity again—the cycle of addiction.

Here's the cycle you've been caught up in: You start using drugs, you get preoccupied with using, your life gets out of control, and then you try to quit but end up using again (relapse).

EXERCISE **3** EXERCISE

Trying to Stop Drinking and Using

➤ How many times have you tried to stop drinking and using? What was it like for you when you tried? Describe one or two of your attempts to stop in the space below.

_____

_____

_____

_____

_____

➤ How long were you able to stop?

_____

➤ Was it easy to stay off alcohol or other drugs?

_____ Yes   _____ No

Why or why not?

_____

_____

_____

➤ What happened when you started using alcohol or other drugs again?

_____

_____

_____

➤ What did you tell yourself when you started using alcohol or other drugs again? What were you thinking?

_____

_____

_____

Screening for Alcohol or Drug Addiction

This exercise describes what happens to people who are addicted to alcohol or other drugs. It will help you see if you are addicted. People who are not addicts do *not* have the problems listed here.

➤ Read each statement. Think back over your life. If this has ever happened to you, make a check mark in the box. If not, leave it blank. It's very important that you answer each honestly. When you are finished, you will add up your score and learn what it means.

☐ 1. **I use in order to feel better.** Sometimes I use alcohol and drugs to get away from feeling things.

☐ 2. **I use in order to deal with problems.** I use alcohol and drugs to deal with many of my problems and to cope with things that bother me.

☐ 3. **It takes more.** It takes more or stronger kinds of alcohol or drugs to get the same feeling as before.

☐ 4. **I have blackouts.** Sometimes after I've been using, I don't remember what happened.

☐ 5. **I sneak drinks or drugs.** Sometimes I hide how much I'm using or drinking. I do this because I don't want people to know or I don't want to share.

☐ 6. **Dependence.** I rarely do anything for fun unless I use alcohol or other drugs.

☐ 7. **I get a fast start.** I use stronger alcohol or drugs or use more quickly at first to get a good start.

☐ 8. **I feel guilty.** I feel guilty about using alcohol or other drugs or about the things I do when I use.

☐ 9. **I don't talk about it.** Other people complain or try to talk to me about my using, but I don't listen.

☐ 10. **I have regular blackouts.** I often don't remember what happened and get into trouble when I use alcohol or other drugs.

☐ 11. **I make excuses.** I use alcohol or other drugs to cope with problems in my life. I have to use to deal with these problems.

☐ 12. **I use more than others.** I use more than most people. I look for people who use as much as or more than I do so I feel that I fit in.

☐ 13. **I feel bad.** I feel bad about how my using hurts other people, but I don't know what to do about it.

☐ 14. **I show off.** I show off or get pushy with other people to feel better, to prove that I'm okay, and to control others.

☐ 15. **I make promises.** I promise myself to get my life in order and do better. I mean it, but it doesn't work out that way.

☐ 16. **I try to control.** I try to control my use or quit, but it doesn't work.

☐ 17. **I give up other things.** I stopped doing things I used to do that didn't involve using alcohol or other drugs.

☐ 18. **I make changes in my life.** I change jobs, move, or leave a relationship to try to make my life better, but it doesn't work.

☐ 19. **I have work and money troubles.** I have problems on the job, owe money, or can't work at all because of my using.

☐ 20. **I avoid friends and family.** I avoid old friends and family who don't use unless I need something from them.

☐ 21. **I neglect food.** I don't eat the proper foods or eat at a regular time, especially when I'm using.

☐ 22. **I feel resentment.** I feel like other people are out to get me, and I feel angry toward them.

☐ 23. **I feel the effects of withdrawal.** I need alcohol or drugs in the morning or I get the shakes or sweats.

☐ 24. **I can't make decisions.** I can't make any decisions, even small ones. I just wait until things happen.

☐ 25. **I have health problems.** I am sick, have lost a lot of weight, or feel physically bad most of the time.

☐ 26. **It takes more to get high.** It takes more for me to get high. No matter how much I use, I can't get the effect I want.

☐ 27. **My behavior is over the line.** I do things I said I would never do or things that do not reflect the way I was raised.

☐ 28. **I use all the time.** I use whenever I can and don't try to have a normal life.

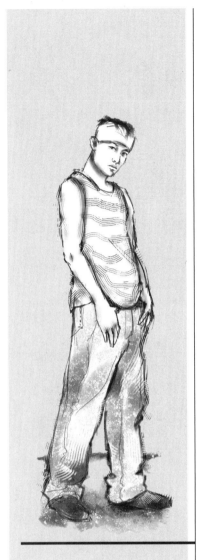

Even when I can't use, I have difficulty thinking, remembering, and doing things that used to be easy.

☐ 29. **I look for people who are worse than me.** I try to use with people who are worse off than I am. It makes me feel better.

☐ 30. **I can't function.** Even when I can't use, I have difficulty thinking, remembering, and doing things that used to be easy.

☐ 31. **I feel afraid.** I feel like something terrible might happen to me, people are out to get me, and I have to be on guard at all times.

☐ 32. **I am giving up.** I don't try to change anything. I just wait to see what happens.

☐ 33. **Nothing else matters.** Getting something to use, using, and getting over using are my whole life.

☐ 34. **I turn to God or a higher power.** I want God or another higher power or some religion to save me from my life.

☐ 35. **I feel lost and alone.** I don't try to pretend my life is normal. I know I am an addict or alcoholic. My life won't change—or can't change.

☐ 36. **I feel totally defeated.** I am willing to do anything to get better.

☐ 37. **I am confined.** I have been incarcerated or in mental health units because of my using.

☐ 38. **I have used while incarcerated.** I have used alcohol or other drugs while incarcerated.

☐ 39. **I have used after treatment during incarceration.** I have been in an addiction treatment program while incarcerated. I started using again after I successfully completed the program.

Add up the number of statements you've checked for each stage of addiction. Write that number in the box next to each stage.

➤ **Early-stage addiction**

Number of boxes checked for questions 1–12: _____

If you have one or more checks in the first section, there is a possibility that you abuse or are addicted to alcohol or other drugs. The closer your score is to 12, the higher your chances of being an addict.

➤ **Middle-stage addiction**

Number of boxes checked for questions 13–24: _____

Any number of checks in this section means that you are addicted and have started to have bad things happen to you because of your addiction. The closer your score is to 12, the more addicted you are and the worse things will get if you don't get help.

➤ **Late-stage addiction**

Number of boxes checked for questions 25–39: _____

Any number of checks in this section means that you are in the late stage of addiction. During this stage, you may have given up hope and thought that you could not do anything to change. Without help, your chances of dying from your addiction are very high if you continue to use alcohol or other drugs.

19

Reactions to the Addiction Screening Test

Answer the questions below honestly. Really think about what work you'll need to do to recover from your drug use.

➤ What do you *think* about the results of your score from exercise 4?

_____

_____

_____

➤ How do you *feel* right now about your score from exercise 4?

_____

_____

_____

➤ What have you just learned about yourself? What are you going to do about it?

_____

_____

_____

_____

_____

It is normal to feel angry or upset about the results of exercise 4. Some people think, "This doesn't mean anything. It's just a bunch of words," and try to ignore the results. This is called denial. Alcoholics and addicts usually deny that they are dependent on alcohol or other drugs. They simply can't think about how to live without their drugs.

➤ Complete the following sentences.

If I don't stop drinking or using, I will probably . . .

_____

_____

_____

If I do stop drinking or using, I might be able to . . .

_____

_____

_____

Alcoholics and addicts usually deny that they are dependent on alcohol or other drugs.

Nine General Symptoms of Addiction

Every illness has symptoms. If you have the flu, for example, the symptoms are coughing, a sore throat, headache, and fever. Addiction also has symptoms. Here are the nine general symptoms of addiction:

1. **Lifestyle oriented to alcohol or other drugs**

   a. Alcohol or other drugs are very important in your life.

   b. You use alone, you look for times to use, and you set up times to use.

   c. You use social drugs as medicines.

   d. You like to be with other alcohol or drug users.

   e. You like to go places where drugs or alcohol will be available.

2. **Mental obsession with alcohol or other drugs**

   a. You spend a lot of time thinking about getting high.

   b. You look forward to times when you can use.

   c. You stockpile your supply of alcohol or other drugs.

3. **Emotional compulsion**

   a. You take drugs or drink alcohol quickly to get high.

   b. You take a lot of drugs or drink a lot of alcohol.

   c. You get uncomfortable and frustrated when you can't use.

4. **Either a low or an overinflated self-image**

   a. You violate your own moral code.

   b. You don't think you're worth anything as a person. (You have low self-esteem.)

   c. You are arrogant; you think you have all the answers, that you're better than everyone.

   d. You often feel hopeless, depressed, and worthless because you don't think you can change.

5. **Rigid negative attitudes**

   a. You are unkind and uncaring to others.

   b. You see the world as a bad place.

   c. You commit crimes.

   d. You don't want to change and act in more positive ways.

6. **Rigid defenses**

   a. You deny your chemical use and its consequences.

   b. You defend, deny, minimize, and rationalize your behaviors.

   c. You won't think about new ways to look at yourself and your behavior.

7. **Delusion**

   a. You can't look at the truth about yourself.

   b. You act unaware of the harmful consequences of alcohol or other drug use.

   c. You act sincere when you say everything is fine, even though it is not.

   d. You can't think about the painful and harmful consequences of your use.

   e. You blame any problems you do see on others.

8. **Powerlessness**

   a. You can't stop your harmful drinking or drug use, even if you can admit that things need to change.

   b. You have lost your ability to manage your own life.

   c. You can't ask for help from others.

   d. You promise to change, but can't.

   e. You change for a short time, but fall back into drinking or using (relapse).

9. **Physical symptoms**

   a. Your body tolerates larger and larger amounts of drugs.

b. You experience withdrawal symptoms when you stop drinking or using drugs.

c. Your memory starts to go bad. You lose track of what happens when you use; or you remember only the good or "high" feelings and forget the harmful consequences.

What drug or drugs you use isn't important. The disease and its consequences are the same. Another important thing about the disease of addiction is that it always gets worse. Always. And if you don't do something about it, *it will kill you.* Fast or slow, the choice is yours. But your addiction *will* kill you. Think about it: You are already incarcerated, locked away from society. Yes, you can make some phone calls to the outside, but you're not free. You're locked up.

Addicts don't make healthy choices. For example, you spend your grocery money on drugs or you rob a store to get money to buy drugs. To make things worse, you ignore or explain away the negative results of your addiction-driven behaviors.

It's also important to understand that *once you are addicted to one drug, you are addicted to all mood-altering substances,* even if you haven't tried them. It's true. Once you are addicted, something changes in your body and in your brain so that when you try another drug, you'll become addicted to that one, too.

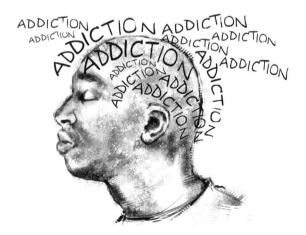

Finding a Trustworthy Person to Sponsor You

You are in a hard spot. You're starting to think about your life. Maybe some of your peers who've been in treatment for a while are pressing you to be more honest with yourself. Maybe you're beginning to doubt the way you've seen yourself.

Trust us on this: You can't make these changes in your life on your own. We have seen many, many people try to do that—and then fail. Needing help from someone doesn't mean you're weak. We all need help sometimes, and it's okay to admit that. A good sponsor will help you in your commitment to change.

Having a good *sponsor* makes all the difference in staying free from drugs and crime. Without a good sponsor, you lessen your chances of success—no matter how much you want it or how hard you work. Remember, you can't do this alone!

Choosing a sponsor is a very important decision. You will tell this person the details of your alcohol and other drug use, your criminal activities, and other information about your life. Your sponsor must be a person you can really trust. This person must also take your behaviors seriously and not play down your chances for relapsing. Your sponsor must be someone you respect and will listen to even if he says something you don't want to hear.

Be careful when choosing your sponsor. You shouldn't choose your girlfriend, spouse, a relative, or someone you might be sexually attracted to. These people are too close to the problem.

Sponsor

Your *sponsor* will be the person you can turn to in a crisis. The one you can call anytime. The person who can give you a kick in the pants when you are making excuses—and give you hope when you are thinking that life just won't ever get better.

A sponsor must be

- sober

- of the same gender

- objective and supportive

- trustworthy

- able to help you find solutions for your problems

- objective and tell you what he thinks, even if you don't want to hear it

A good sponsor believes that abstinence is the only solution for addicts and is active in a recovery program. Examples of recovery programs are Alcoholics Anonymous, Narcotics Anonymous, Men for Sobriety, 13 Feathers, and Walking the Red Road.

A sponsor must be someone you truly respect, not for how much money he has or for his nice car, but as a person.

Sponsors have jobs. They have families and care about them and other people. They don't rob, steal, or do drugs. They've earned the respect of their family, friends, and community. They do things for others. It's how they "give back."

While you are still incarcerated, ask your counselor for advice on who could be your sponsor. This person might be a senior peer in your program. Some recovery programs like AA can get you a sponsor while you are incarcerated. When you are released, this person might continue to be your sponsor.

Having a good sponsor makes all the difference in staying free from drugs and crime.

Choosing a Sponsor

➤ Make a list of the people in your life who could be your sponsor. In the space provided, write the reasons for and against that person being a good sponsor. Consider the qualities this person has, like being truthful, trustworthy, caring, able to keep secrets, and so forth. Your sponsor should also meet the guidelines on page 26. This person should also have the time to help you and strongly believe that your only hope is no drug use or criminal activity.

____ Person: _____

Reasons **for** being a good sponsor: _____

_____

_____

Reasons **against** being a good sponsor: _____

_____

_____

____ Person: _____

Reasons **for** being a good sponsor: _____

_____

_____

Reasons **against** being a good sponsor: _____

_____

_____

_____ Person: _____

Reasons **for** being a good sponsor: _____

_____

_____

Reasons **against** being a good sponsor: _____

_____

_____

_____ Person: _____

Reasons **for** being a good sponsor: _____

_____

_____

Reasons **against** being a good sponsor: _____

_____

_____

➤ Rank the people on your list from the best to least acceptable choice. (Number one should be the best, number two the second best, and so on.) Choose the top three people. Talk with your group about each of them.

➤ Ask your support group or therapist which person, if any, would work best as your sponsor and why. If none of the people are going to work out, start a new list in your notebook.

Once you choose a sponsor, talk with your group leader about exactly how to start your sponsor relationship. One of the results of your drug use and addiction is that you become isolated. Over time, you have slowly cut yourself off from family and friends. No matter who you choose as a sponsor, you must tell this person *everything*. If you edit, omit, or filter information, you will limit how effective your treatment is. The key to success is sharing everything—even your very worst secrets. It's okay to admit how out of control you have been.

After you tell your story to one person, you may feel so relieved that you want to tell more people. That's not a good idea. Right now, telling one person who can help you set up a plan for dealing with this problem is enough. Later, you can tell other people—but talk with your counselor or group leader before you do.

Miguel's Story (continued)

In the past, I didn't trust anyone. To stay sober and clean, I finally realized that I needed to trust people. My sponsor is an ex-con, which proved to be a major help. But I only get out of this relationship what I put in. This means taking the risk to ask questions, writing and calling him, speaking out at meetings, and making daily contact. Without my sponsor, I'm not sure I'd still be sober.

— Miguel, incarcerated
A New Direction program participant

Your Body on Alcohol and Other Drugs

What happens to your body when you are addicted? While the process is complicated, the basic ideas are simple to understand.

First, your brain uses chemical and electrical energy to send and receive messages to and from the rest of your body. Pain, temperature, danger, and hunger are examples of this. When your stomach is empty, your brain gets a signal that your body needs food. A message is sent to your stomach. You then feel hunger.

The Pleasure Pathway

Body functions like breathing and heartbeat are controlled by certain areas of the brain. Other parts of the brain respond to pain or pleasure. Here's how it works:

1. Most of your good feelings come from an area in the brain known as the "pleasure pathway." When something good happens to you, your brain makes chemicals that make you feel happy.

2. The pleasure pathway is also where drugs like alcohol and cocaine affect the brain. They give you an extra burst of pleasurable feelings.

3. These feelings do not last.

4. The natural level of your brain's own chemicals for making you feel happy drop when these mood-changing chemicals leave your body.

5. You then feel uncomfortable, sad, depressed, or nervous.

6. During withdrawal, the more drugs you've been using, the worse you feel. Your body is reacting to not having its drugs.

7. You don't like these feelings, so you take more drugs to get high so you feel better again.

You need alcohol or other drugs just to feel okay. Your brain and body are now "addicted" to these drugs. Soon, getting drugs to feel okay becomes the most important thing in your life. That's all you want to do.

The Addicted Brain

The brains of addicted people are different from the brains of people who aren't addicted. Drugs like alcohol, cocaine, meth, and marijuana affect addicted people differently. "Normal" people do not experience the intense "high" that addicts love so much.

At some point in an addict's history of drinking or using, a change takes place in the person's brain. This change makes the addict want to use drugs again and again despite negative results.

Once the change happens in your body to make you an addict, you can't ever go back to "normal." Remember the story about the cucumber turning into a pickle in part 1? This is the way it is even if you stop drinking and using drugs for years.

When you start *any* drug use again, the cycle begins again. This is how we know that addiction is a disease. Once the chemistry of addiction takes place, it can never be cured.

Once the chemistry of addiction takes place, it can never be cured.

It can only be stopped by not using the drug and having a good recovery program.

This is one of the main causes of relapse: After you haven't used for a while, you feel healthy. You feel good. You think you're cured. You think you can handle drugs again. But you can't.

Relapse = Incarceration or Death

When you try to stop using drugs, you just won't feel quite right. This is withdrawal. Your body has become adjusted to the drugs you were using. While your brain and body heal, you can feel not quite right for a while. It will take some time for your brain to learn to make its own "good feeling" chemicals again *without* drugs. To help your brain get better faster, get enough exercise, sleep, and share your feelings with others. (This will be discussed in greater detail later.)

Recovery isn't about how not to use drugs.
It's about learning how to live comfortably
without having to turn to them.

EXERCISE 7 EXERCISE

What Are Feelings?

➤ Think back to a time when you were not using alcohol or other drugs (but weren't in treatment, either). Maybe you stopped because your family was on your case or someone had threatened to leave you. Or maybe you were just trying to prove to yourself that you could control your use. In the space below, describe your thoughts and feelings at the time.

_____

_____

_____

_____

_____

Three Major Classes of Drugs

The three major classes of drugs are

- depressants

- stimulants

- stimulant-depressants

The drugs in each of these classes have many harmful physical side effects.

Depressants

Depressants, or downers, are drugs that slow down your brain activity. The entire body just slows down. Slurred speech, poor coordination, slow reflexes and reaction time, sleepiness, confusion, and slowed breathing are symptoms of using these drugs.

Depressants include the following:

- alcohol

- Quaaludes

- tranquilizers like Valium, Xanax, Librium, and Klonapin

- barbiturates such as Seconal and Tuinal

- sleeping pills like Dalmane and Halcion

If you've used alcohol, you might be thinking, "Hey, when I drink, I feel *great!* Alcohol isn't a downer; it gets me up! It gets me *high.*" Yes, that's the first effect of alcohol. But as you drink more and more, what happens? You fall asleep. You pass out. And *that's* because alcohol is a depressant. There's a short high, but as you keep drinking, your body slows down more and more. Your breathing can even stop, resulting in death.

Medical Effects of Depressants, Including Alcohol
Alcohol is the most often abused drug in the United States, and it is the *most dangerous* drug of abuse because it affects *every* organ of the body. No body part is safe from its harmful effects.

- Alcohol poisons all of your body's organs and systems. It irritates the lining of the stomach and intestines, causing nausea, vomiting, and diarrhea.

- Alcohol is also one of the causes of intestine, stomach, mouth, and throat cancer.

- Alcohol destroys your liver. It becomes swollen and stops working right. If you drink long enough, scars form in your liver and cause the liver to fail completely.

- Alcohol has major effects on your heart and blood vessels. Drinking three or more drinks a day can raise your blood pressure and increase your risk of heart attack or heart failure.

- Drinking alcohol causes the air tubes in your lungs to become narrower, making it difficult to breathe.

- Nearly all alcoholics suffer some brain damage as a result of drinking. Alcohol affects your memory and your ability to think.

- Alcohol lowers your sex drive as well as your ability to have sex.

- Children born to alcoholic mothers can have severe medical problems, including heart defects, low intelligence, and mental retardation.

- Alcoholics are often more depressed and have a higher rate of suicide than most people.

Withdrawal from alcohol and other depressants is extremely dangerous. If left untreated, withdrawal can cause seizures and death. *By far, alcohol and other depressant drugs are the most dangerous substances that addicts use.*

Other depressants—including tranquilizers, barbiturates, and sleeping pills—act on the brain just like alcohol. They do not cause liver damage or high blood pressure, but their effects are still dangerous.

Physical Effects of Alcohol
or Other Depressants

➤ How has alcohol or other depressants affected you physically? Common medical problems of people who abuse alcohol are listed below. Place an **X** next to each problem you've had.

____ high blood pressure that was hard for my doctor to treat

____ morning nausea, vomiting, shakes, dizziness

____ morning cough

____ heart attacks

____ frequent stomach pain, bleeding

____ being told by an emergency room doctor to change my lifestyle of drugs and crime because it is going to kill me

____ abnormal liver tests due to alcohol

____ frequent broken bones, unexplained bruises, and fights

____ difficulty remembering what I did while drinking (blackouts)

____ hospital stay for any problem caused by my drinking, such as broken bones or fights

____ being told by my doctor that I had a health problem caused by drinking

____ vomiting blood as a result of drinking

➤ Other effects:

_____

_____

Stimulants

Caffeine, nicotine, cocaine, crack, methamphetamine, crystal, and amphetamines are all *stimulants,* or uppers. All stimulants intensify brain and body functions—they speed things up. These effects last for short periods of time, usually five to thirty minutes. Stimulants also use up specific brain chemicals. Without these chemicals, the craving for more stimulants is very strong.

With stimulants, the addictive process starts early and happens quickly.

Crack and nicotine are the two most addictive drugs. People can become addicted to crack after a few hits. The first hit is always the best; chase it as you might, you can never experience it again. Most stimulants don't stay in the body very long. So you have to take them over and over again.

Medical Effects of Stimulants

Most health problems caused by stimulants occur during drug use. Amphetamines and cocaine cause high blood pressure and rapid heartbeat. Regardless of age, cocaine users risk heart attack.

Brain damage often happens to people who use cocaine and amphetamines. Cocaine users can have seizures during use. If not treated, seizures will continue—sometimes killing the user. Stimulants can also cause brain damage and even death from strokes.

Stimulants decrease the normal human drive for sleep, sex, and food. Heavy stimulant users are often malnourished. Problems connected to poor diet can cause other body damage, especially to the brain.

Injecting stimulants with dirty or shared needles causes other problems. Infections and abscesses on the skin where you inject are common. HIV and hepatitis are also spread by injecting drugs.

Most stimulants don't stay in the body very long. So you have to take them over and over again.

Stimulants are very addicting and dangerous. Since many of these drugs are illegal, they are frequently connected with violent crime. Many users die as a result of the drug use or from the lifestyle related to it.

EXERCISE **9** EXERCISE

Effects of Stimulants

➤ How has stimulant use affected your health? Here is a list of complications from using stimulants. Place an **X** next to each one you've experienced.

____ feeling like my heart was going to jump right out of my chest

____ hole formed inside nose

____ tweaking

____ chest pain

____ seizures while using

____ loose teeth

____ joint pain

____ seeing or hearing things that were not there (hallucinations)

____ violent behavior (while using)

____ decreased ability to think

____ malnourishment because of "binges" of stimulant use

____ seeing and feeling "coke bugs"

____ believing that people are "after me" or following me while using (paranoia)

____ feeling that I can't trust anyone (paranoia)

____ peeping out of windows

____ having children born with birth defects due to my stimulant use

➤ Other effects:

_____

_____

➤ Next, list the people you know who have died from or are very sick from using stimulants.

_____

_____

_____

_____

Stimulant–Depressants

Certain drugs act as both stimulants and depressants. These drugs first speed up and then slow down your body's functions. Narcotics, hallucinogens, and inhalants are stimulant-depressants.

Narcotics

Morphine, heroin, codeine, Darvon, Dilaudid, Talwin, Vicodin, and methadone are narcotics. These drugs relieve pain and increase pleasure in your body. The harmful effects of narcotics include constipation, nausea, and vomiting, decreased interest in sex, extreme hunger, low blood pressure, slowed breathing, sleepiness, and loss of interest in normal activities.

A common danger with narcotics is poor drug quality because street narcotics are uncontrolled. Dealers, as you know, can "cut" narcotics however they want and with whatever they want. You can die from poisonous substances in the drug or from taking a drug, like heroin, that is more pure than your body can handle.

Hallucinogens

Hallucinogens include LSD, PCP (angel dust), mescaline, peyote, marijuana, and "club drugs" like ecstasy, GHB, and ketamine. These drugs greatly increase a chemical in the brain that provides a sense of well-being. This causes hallucinations. Some of these drugs, particularly PCP, can cause extreme strength and violence. After the effects of these drugs wear off, depression and tiredness set in. These drugs are often cut with other chemicals that are poisonous.

Inhalants

Inhalants include glues, paint thinners, nail polish remover, gasoline, benzene, and nitrous oxide. These drugs are very dangerous because death or brain damage can happen with only one use. Craziness and hallucinations, confusion, nausea, vomiting, headaches, seizures, and heart attacks are the effects. Inhalants damage your liver, kidneys, and bone marrow. Even small doses can cause cancer. Worse yet, the younger you are when you use, the greater the damage you do to your body. This is because young, growing cells are more easily damaged than the cells in an adult's body.

Marijuana

While marijuana is included in the hallucinogens category, many people think that marijuana is a harmless, non-addictive drug. That's simply not the case. Marijuana is a huge problem for many people. It has many of the same side effects as other hallucinogens and is often the gateway to other drug use. Long-term side effects include memory loss and decreased ability to learn.

Effects of Stimulant-Depressant Drugs

➤ A list of some of the effects caused by using stimulant-depressant drugs follows. Place an **X** next to each effect you have experienced during your drug use.

Narcotic effects

____ severe nausea and vomiting from drugs

____ regular constipation

____ overdose

____ auto accidents due to "nodding off" from narcotics

____ a girlfriend or wife who had a baby with birth defects due to drugs

____ a girlfriend or wife who had a baby that needed withdrawal from narcotics at birth

____ hallucinations (seeing things that weren't really there)

____ violent behavior while on drugs

____ decreased interest in sex while taking drugs

Marijuana effects

____ poor memory

____ lack of motivation (for work or school)

____ problems with learning

____ trouble with thinking and problem-solving

____ sterility (can't father a child)

____ deformed sperm

____ poor concentration

____ coughing

____ increased lung cancer risk

____ weakened immune system

____ sore throat

General effects of stimulant-depressants

____ constant headaches

____ admission to a mental hospital for symptoms caused by drug use

____ brain damage from inhalants or hallucinogens

____ "bad trips"

____ kidney or liver damage

____ flashbacks

➤ Other effects:

_____

_____

_____

How have drugs influenced you physically, mentally, emotionally, and psychologically?

How many effects can you relate to? By reviewing the list of the effects of different drugs, you should be able to get a better idea how these drugs have influenced you physically, mentally, emotionally, and psychologically.

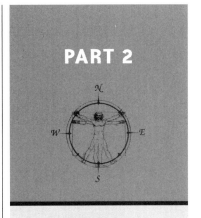

The Disease of Addiction and Its Effects

Addiction to alcohol and other drugs was once seen as a moral problem. Addicts were thought to be weak willed. We thought that they just didn't care enough about other people or themselves to quit. We'd say, "Why don't they just control their drinking like the rest of us do?"

43

Today, we know you can't "just quit." It's not possible. Addicts are often the last to realize they are sick with a deadly illness. And your family and friends also find it hard to face addiction. In fact, they might be addicts, too. Like anyone suffering from a serious illness, you need help.

Features of Addiction

Here are the six major parts of the disease of addiction:

1. **It's an illness.** Addiction to alcohol or other drugs is an illness with clear symptoms, such as blackouts, preoccupation with use, increased drug tolerance, and shakes.

2. **It's chronic.** Once an alcoholic/drug addict, always an alcoholic/drug addict. Once you turn into a pickle, you can't go back to being a cucumber. You will never be able to use "normally" again.

3. **It's progressive.** This disease will get worse and worse unless it is treated. If you stop drinking or using for months or even years but then begin drinking or using again, you will be right back where you left off in a very short time.

4. **It causes "social" death.** Eventually, you will be removed from your community and incarcerated like you are now. There are many routes to incarceration—vehicular homicide, dealing or buying illegal drugs, violence while under the influence, and more. Regardless of the path you're on, all drug-using paths for addicts lead to social and physical death.

5. **It will kill you.** If you are an alcoholic or drug addict who continues to drink or use, your drug use will eventually kill you (and maybe someone else, too). Death may result from accidents,

suicide, overdoses, murder, or the destruction
of your body by these drugs and drug lifestyle.
Addiction will kill you. It's only a matter of
time. You can count on it.

6. **Not drinking/using is the only cure.**
The only effective addiction treatment is to
stop using and to form a new group of people
who can help and support your new, drug-free
life. Is it easy? No. Is it possible? Yes! Millions
and millions of people have recovered from this
disease. You can, too.

Keep these points in mind:

• If the use of alcohol or other drugs causes *any*
regular trouble in your life and *you do not stop
using,* you're addicted.

• A person who is not an alcoholic, for example, might
have one drunk driving offense. He might have one
alcohol-related problem at work. He might have
family problems because of one drinking episode.
But one problem—just one—would be enough
to make him say, "If I'm going to have
this kind of trouble, I'm going to
stop using this now!" And then
he quits.

• An alcoholic or addict like you,
on the other hand, keeps on
drinking or using even though
it causes problem after problem.
Blaming problems on family,
friends, work, society, police,
and courts is not useful.
Drinking or using becomes
more important than
anything else.

The chart on the next page shows the symptoms of addiction from the early stage of this disease through its final stage. As we have said, this is a progressive disease. Review the answers you gave in the Screening for Alcohol or Drug Addiction on pages 15–19 of part 1. Also note the symptoms under each stage of addiction on the next page. Place an **X** next to the stage that you can most relate to.

The Effects of Your Addiction

So far you have learned about what addiction is. You've seen what alcohol and other drugs do to your body. The impact of your drug use goes far beyond just your body. Your drug use has affected many other people in ways you never imagined.

How far do the effects of your drug use extend? Picture a perfectly calm lake. What happens when you throw a stone into that lake? Ripples shoot out from the spot where the stone hit the water. And they go on and on past the point where you can no longer even see them.

In a way, your drug use is like a stone hitting the water of the lives around you. The effects of your use spread out away from you like the ripple in that lake. Your use affects everyone you know—your wife or lover, children, parents, grandparents, brothers, sisters, friends, and other people in your neighborhood, state, and country. This might be really hard to believe. But it is true. As you continue in this workbook, you'll begin the very important step of looking at the harmful consequences of your drug use. And that means looking at how your use has affected the lives of everyone you know—and even people you'll never meet.

Figure 1

PERSONALIZED ADDICTION DISEASE CHART (ADAPTED FROM THE JELLINEK CURVE)

Early Stage

___ Sneaks drinks or other drugs

___ Is preoccupied with alcohol or other drugs

___ Gulps drinks/rapidly uses drugs

___ Avoids reference to alcohol or other drug use

___ Has memory blackouts

___ Has increased tolerance for alcohol or other drugs

___ Drinks or uses before and after social occasions

___ Begins using alcohol or other drugs for relief of tension, stress, etc.

___ Is uncomfortable in situations without alcohol or other drugs

Middle Stage

___ Experiences loss of control

___ Is dishonest about use of alcohol or other drugs

___ Uses alcohol or other drugs for relief of tension and stress more and more often

___ Hides and protects supply of alcohol or other drugs

___ Has urgent need for the day's first use of alcohol or other drugs

___ Tries periods of forced abstinence

___ Others disapprove of use of alcohol or other drugs

___ Rationalizes use of alcohol or other drugs

___ Becomes more and more aggressive

___ Shows grandiose behavior

___ Feels guilty about use of alcohol or other drugs

___ Eats poorly and sometimes "forgets" to eat

___ Builds unreasonable resentments

___ Cares less and less about personal relationships

___ Considers moving to a new neighborhood or city to cure use of alcohol or other drugs

___ Sexual drive becomes less and less

___ Quits or loses jobs

___ Becomes more and more jealous of others

___ Uses alcohol or other drugs alone (secretly)

___ Tries to control use of alcohol or other drugs

Late Stage

___ Begins to have tremors and shakes

___ Drinks or uses other drugs in the early morning

___ Begins to feel sad more and more of the time

___ Has long binges of using alcohol or other drugs

___ Can't think clearly anymore

___ Loses tolerance for use of alcohol or other drugs

___ Begins to feel generally afraid more and more often

___ Cannot work

___ Physical health gets worse and worse

___ Moral standards are lost

___ Is admitted to a hospital or treatment center

___ Loses family and friends

___ Runs out of excuses for using alcohol or other drugs

Final Stage

___ Incarceration and/or death

Earlier, you saw how addicts regularly give up control of themselves. As an addict, you lose the ability to make good choices. You also ignore or explain away the harmful results of your addictive behaviors.

Most addicts don't realize for a long time that they are addicted. You may be thinking the same thing—that you're not an addict. This is one of the biggest problems with addiction. It's like a vise that closes very slowly. You ignore it until there's no way to escape.

Addictive behavior develops slowly. That's one reason you don't see it coming. You may have smoked your first joint because others were doing it. Maybe it just seemed like a good idea at the time. It felt good, so you tried it again. Soon, you began to buy your own stash. It became part of your life. You made sure you had it with you at school, work, vacations, or concerts. You began to deal dope, too.

After a while, you began "pampering" your addiction. You started to choose friends who also liked to get high. You developed a whole ritual around smoking. A favorite pipe, a certain brand of rolling papers, a roach clip on your key chain, a stash box for your dope and equipment, and a special way of cleaning the pot all became part of the ritual. Slowly these rituals become such a part of your life that you no longer think about it. One day, you realize that the first thing you do in the morning and the last thing you do at night is light up a joint. And you spend more and more time getting high or trying to get alcohol or other drugs.

*"**Addiction** is like a thief in the night! Sometimes it takes a little, sometimes a lot, but it never gets enough. It keeps coming back for more until it owns you . . . all of you."*

— Anonymous inmate

Criminal and Addiction History

The first step in recovery is to recognize your addiction and criminal history—and how they are related. As a criminal and addictive thinker, you might say, "I haven't got a problem. I'm fine." You deny that alcohol or other drugs are a problem for you. You deny that you like the rush of excitement of doing forbidden things. You even deny the harmful consequences of your criminal lifestyle and addiction (or blame them on someone else). But your using behaviors *have* affected you and other people around you. As you continue in this workbook, you will look more closely at this.

There are many ways addicts and criminals think and behave when using alcohol or other drugs or committing crimes. Some want to fight or argue, feel sorry for themselves, or blame others for their problems. Some go off by themselves, abandoning their family and friends. Others become very aggressive and victimize and hurt others. Some criminals and addicts do all of this and more! Changing these behavior patterns will lead to sobriety and physical and spiritual freedom. In this workbook you'll learn how to make these changes.

Right now you need to focus on where you've been so you can find out how you got where you are right now—locked up.

Your Criminal History

➤ The first step to honesty and recovery is admitting to and taking responsibility for your criminal past. List every crime you've been arrested and convicted for. Write the year of the offense after each listing.

For some of you, this will be a long list. If necessary, complete this exercise in a notebook. List your crimes in order, from your most recent all the way back to your first crime.

Crime   Year

1. _____ _____

2. _____ _____

3. _____ _____

4. _____ _____

5. _____ _____

6. _____ _____

➤ How much time have you spent locked up for these offenses?

_____ years   _____ months

➤ What is the longest time you have spent crime free?

_____ years   _____ months

➤ Now think about all the crimes you've committed that you never got caught for. How many crimes do you guess you've done that you were never arrested or convicted for?

_____

➤ Over the course of your life, how much time and energy have you spent thinking about ways to make illegal money—make a quick score—or do some other type of crime?

Check one.

☐   I spend almost all my time and energy that way.

☐   I spend much of my time and energy that way.
(50 percent or more)

☐   I spend some time and energy that way.
(less than 50 percent)

☐   I never spend time or energy thinking about crime.

➤ Look at the list of your crimes on page 50. Did they happen more and more often or did they seem to go in "bursts" (a lot of crime followed by a cooling-off period followed by a lot of crime again)?

_____

_____

_____

➤ What patterns do you see in your criminal activity throughout your life?

_____

_____

_____

_____

➤ What crimes did you commit while under the influence of alcohol or other drugs?

_____

_____

_____

_____

_____

➤ What crimes did you commit while *not* under the influence of alcohol or other drugs?

_____

_____

_____

_____

_____

➤ What crimes did you commit while trying to get alcohol or other drugs?

_____

_____

_____

_____

_____

➤ Did you ever switch to different types of crimes? (check one)

_____ Yes   _____ No

If so, why did you switch, and when?

_____

_____

_____

_____

_____

The first step to honesty and recovery is admitting to and taking responsibility for your criminal past.

➤ Were most of your crimes committed on the spur of the moment, or did you think them through first? For example, did you ever steal just for the thrill of it? Give some examples of how you planned or didn't plan crimes from your own criminal history.

1. _____

_____

_____

_____

_____

2. _____

_____

_____

_____

_____

3. _____

_____

_____

_____

_____

➤ List three examples of why you think your criminal behavior is out of control. This may include wanting to stop but doing it anyway, committing crimes even when you didn't care if you got caught, committing crime for the fun of it, and so on. In each of the three examples, describe the crime itself and how it seemed out of control.

1. _____

   _____

   _____

   _____

   _____

2. _____

   _____

   _____

   _____

   _____

3. _____

   _____

   _____

   _____

   _____

➤ For you, what have been the five worst consequences of your criminal behavior?

1. _____

2. _____

3. _____

4. _____

5. _____

➤ For your family, friends, and victims, what have been the consequences of your criminal behavior?

1. _____

2. _____

3. _____

4. _____

5. _____

➤ Give five reasons why criminal behavior and a criminal lifestyle seemed attractive to you.

1. _____

   _____

   _____

2. _____

   _____

   _____

3. _____

   _____

   _____

4. _____

   _____

   _____

5. _____

   _____

   _____

"I started using weed when I was sixteen. I used it heavily for 10 years. When I quit, it was like I had been asleep for all those years. Nothing had changed. I had almost no memory of all those years."

— Tommy L.,
  burglary, 7 years,
  St. Brides Correctional Center,
  Virginia
  (Free at Last)

Your Addiction History

Just as with your criminal history, the first step to honesty and recovery from your addiction is admitting your chemical history. List every type of drug you have used to get high, as far back as you can remember. After listing each drug, write the year you first used it and the year you most recently used it.

Again, for some of you, this will be a long list. If necessary, complete this exercise in a notebook. **Note:** List each drug only once. Don't list every single time you got high on the drug—just the first and most recent time you used it.

▶ Drug

Drug	Year of first use	Year of most recent use
_____	_____	_____
_____	_____	_____
_____	_____	_____
_____	_____	_____
_____	_____	_____
_____	_____	_____
_____	_____	_____
_____	_____	_____
_____	_____	_____

➤ What are your drugs of choice? Just before your most recent arrest, how much did you use of each in a typical week?

      Drug   Amount used each week

1. _____ _____

2. _____ _____

3. _____ _____

4. _____ _____

➤ Did you ever have trouble concentrating because you day-dreamed about using alcohol or other drugs? (check one)

_____ Yes _____ No

If so, how often did this happen? (circle one)

      Rarely   Often   Constantly

➤ Did your use of alcohol or other drugs increase or decrease over time? If it increased, how? What time in your life was your use the heaviest?

_____

_____

_____

_____

➤ Give five reasons why using alcohol or other drugs seemed attractive to you.

1. _____

_____

2. _____

_____

3. _____

_____

4. _____

_____

5. _____

_____

The first step to honesty and recovery from your addiction is admitting your chemical history.

➤ Did you ever switch from one drug to another? (check one)

_____ Yes   _____ No

Why or why not?

_____

_____

_____

➤ Did you ever move to another neighborhood, city, or state to escape the consequences of your alcohol or other drug use or to "get a fresh start"? Explain.

_____

_____

_____

➤ Did you hide your drug of choice? If so, why and from whom? How did you protect your supply?

_____

_____

_____

➤ Have you ever **blacked out** or overdosed taking drugs or drinking? List examples.

_____

_____

_____

_____

_____

_____

Blackout

A *blackout* is when a person under the influence of alcohol or other drugs continues to function but has no memory afterward of what happened. A blackout is not passing out; it is a period of time when you cannot recall what happened.

➤ List four examples of abuse that you committed while you were high. The types of abuse are physical, emotional, verbal, and sexual.

1. _____

_____

_____

2. _____

_____

_____

3. _____

_____

_____

4. _____

_____

_____

➤ Have you ever felt bad about things you did while you were high? Explain.

_____

_____

_____

➤ Do you think your addiction has gotten out of control?
List five examples of how it may be out of control. These
may include wanting to stop but using anyway, seeking out
drugs even though you knew it was dangerous, committing
crimes only because you needed to get high, and so on.
Describe each incident and how it seemed out of control.

1. _____

_____

_____

2. _____

_____

_____

3. _____

_____

_____

4. _____

_____

_____

5. _____

_____

_____

➤ For you, what have been the five worst consequences of your use of alcohol or other drugs?

1. _____

_____

2. _____

_____

3. _____

_____

4. _____

_____

5. _____

_____

➤ For your family and friends, what have been the consequences of your use of alcohol or other drugs?

1. _____

_____

2. _____

_____

3. _____

_____

4. _____

_____

5. _____

_____

➤ Have you ever promised or tried to stop using alcohol or other drugs? Explain.

_____

_____

_____

➤ What is the longest time you have been sober (not used alcohol or other drugs) since you started using?

_____

➤ Why did you try to sober up?

_____

_____

➤ Why did you start using again?

_____

_____

➤ Have you ever been in drug or alcohol treatment before?
List each place of treatment and whether you were forced
to enter or you entered of your own free will. List your
treatments in order, from your most recent back to your
first treatment. State whether you completed them.

Treatment place	Year	Forced?	Completed?
_____	_____	_____	_____
_____	_____	_____	_____
_____	_____	_____	_____
_____	_____	_____	_____
_____	_____	_____	_____
_____	_____	_____	_____
_____	_____	_____	_____
_____	_____	_____	_____
_____	_____	_____	_____

Powerlessness

Powerlessness is not being able to stop using alcohol or other drugs no matter how hard you try and no matter what happens as a result of your use. It means your use is out of your control. Once you start drinking or using, you don't want to stop. You can't stop.

You may not like the idea that there is some part of your life that you don't have power over. This is natural because you've spent most of your life telling yourself that you are in control—of your life and of the lives of others.

Now is the time to *really* take a hard look at yourself, especially your drug use. Are you really in control? Stop and think. How have you tried to stop, cut back, set limits on, or change the types of alcohol or other drugs that you use? Maybe you'd stopped drinking or using at work. Or maybe you promised yourself you'd use only at night, on weekends, or only with friends, but never alone. But what happened?

Think about your preoccupation with alcohol or other drugs and criminal behavior. Are you drinking or using as a way to reduce anxiety in your life?

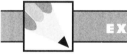 EXERCISE **13** EXERCISE

Looking at Your Thinking

➤ How have your thinking and activities revolved around your use of alcohol or other drugs?

_____

_____

_____

_____

The simple fact is that you have *not* been able to control your drinking and drug use. You probably told yourself you could stop anytime. But you haven't, because you can't—at least not until you ended up incarcerated. That's powerlessness. Think about it. Preoccupation and powerlessness involve planning your day around your use, daydreaming about it, and getting anxious and angry when something prevents you from using.

Your attempts to control your use of alcohol or other drugs show that your use is already out of control. If it wasn't out of control, you wouldn't need to think about it!

Powerlessness *means that you use even if you don't want to. You may even tell yourself, "Don't use. I don't want to use. Don't use, you'll get in trouble." But you* **still** *use.*

EXERCISE **14** EXERCISE

Powerlessness Inventory

➤ It's time to do a powerlessness inventory. List examples that show how powerless you were to stop your drinking and other drug use. Be clear about what you've done to control your use and how often. For example: "I said that I'm only going to use on weekends." "I said that I'll only use at parties and with friends, but not at home by myself."

1. _____

   _____

2. _____

   _____

3. _____

_____

4. _____

_____

➤ Unplanned use can happen in many ways. For example, maybe you planned to visit your son but got high instead. Perhaps you didn't want to get high with friends before you went to see your grandmother, but you did anyway. Or you used when you were incarcerated because of peer pressure.

List times when your unplanned use happened.

_____

_____

_____

_____

➤ Give more examples of powerlessness and loss of control over your use of alcohol or other drugs.

_____

_____

_____

_____

Your attempts to control your use of alcohol or other drugs show that your use is already out of control.

Unmanageability

Unmanageability and powerlessness are closely connected. Unmanageability grows out of powerlessness. When you can't stop using alcohol or other drugs, it affects all parts of your life.

Eventually, your life is unmanageable. *Unmanageable* means that alcohol or drug use has made your life crazy. Your life becomes a disaster. Things just start falling apart. For example:

- You rob a store to get money for drugs even though you could get caught and do serious time.

- You are kicked out of your house. You are told to never come back and stay away from your kids because you're a bad influence.

- You keep driving even though you have no license, you've had three DUIs, and you will be incarcerated if you get caught driving.

- You spend all your family's money on drugs even though you know that there will be nothing left for food or rent.

Miguel's Story (continued)

Eventually, I learned that one of the biggest obstacles to change and recovery was my ego. Our egos won't let us admit that we have no control over people, places, and things. Until I admitted this to myself, I was fighting a losing battle. When the guard yelled "lock-up," I had to confront my powerlessness. Looking through the bars on a beautiful day when I wanted to be on the outside made me understand powerlessness. Refusing to admit my lack of control over addiction will doom me to a lifetime of misery. Addiction is the only war in which you have to surrender to win.

— Miguel, incarcerated
A New Direction program participant

Unmanageability Inventory

➤ Describe the first time you noted that your alcohol or other drug use was becoming unmanageable.

_____

_____

_____

_____

_____

➤ List other ways your life has become unmanageable because of your drug or alcohol use and criminal behavior? Job? Health? Family? Money? The law?

_____

_____

_____

_____

_____

Consequences

There are two parts to the danger of addiction and the damage it causes:

1. the effect on you
2. the effect of your behavior on other people and society

Your addictive behaviors affected the lives of many, many people. Drug addiction can eat up an entire family's budget. Getting caught with drugs and then being incarcerated takes you away from your partner and children for many years. It also forces them to support themselves without your help.

Addictive behaviors hurt society—for example, when an alcoholic becomes violent and attacks a stranger or injures someone in a car accident, when a crack user robs someone for money to buy more drugs, or when an HIV-positive addict shares needles with others or has unprotected sex.

Like most addicts, you think that everyone will overlook or forget the damage caused by what you've done. And you've probably been angry when this didn't happen.

Consequences, however, can be signs that point to reality. The world does not share an addict's distorted thoughts. Lies, broken promises, and selfish behavior will eventually cost, and cost dearly.

> *"**You** get to choose your behavior,*
> *but the **world** chooses the consequences."*
>
> —Anonymous

As long as you tell yourself you don't have a problem with alcohol or other drugs, you will keep having negative consequences. After incarceration, though, the moment of truth arrives. You are in the middle of a disaster. When you stop and look at the results of your use of alcohol and other drugs and criminal behavior, you see just how you and many others have been affected. Though it is difficult to face the "wreckage of your past," as Alcoholics Anonymous puts it, an honest look at your consequences will greatly improve your chances of getting free from drugs and criminal behavior forever.

The Effects of Alcohol or Other Drug Use on Your Life

Physical Condition

Consider how using alcohol and other drugs may have affected you physically:

- continuing addictive behavior despite the risk to your health

- extreme weight loss or gain

- physical problems, such as ulcers or high blood pressure

- physical injury or abuse by others

- involvement in abusive or dangerous situations

- vehicle accidents
  (car, motorcycle, boat, ATV, snowmobile)

- injury to yourself from your sexual behavior

- sleep disturbances
  (not enough sleep, too much sleep)

- lack of energy/physical exhaustion

Physical Effects of Using

➤ List examples of how your use of alcohol or other drugs affected you physically.

1. _____

2. _____

3. _____

4. _____

5. _____

Thinking Processes

When you put chemicals in your body that have an effect on your brain, those drugs affect your thinking, too. When you are drinking or using, you don't think clearly. As a result, you make unhealthy and irrational decisions.

Unhealthy Choices Made While Drinking or Using

➤ Think of examples of unhealthy choices you made while using drugs (such as getting drunk and smashing a car window, robbing a liquor store, spending your family's food money on drugs). List them on the next page.

1. _____

2. _____

3. _____

4. _____

5. _____

➤ Would you have made these choices if you hadn't been drinking or using? Explain why or why not.

_____

_____

_____

➤ What problems of yours did you blame on others?

_____

_____

_____

➤ Would you want your children, sister, or brother to make the same kind of decisions? Explain.

_____

_____

_____

Financial Effects

There are obvious financial costs to using alcohol or other drugs. There are also expenses that are not so easy to see. You may be surprised at what the actual cost of your drug use has been.

EXERCISE **18** EXERCISE

Financial Costs of Drinking or Using

➤ How much money did you spend each week on drugs or alcohol?

$ _____

Multiply this amount by 52 to see how much you spent in a year.

$ _____ x 52 = $ _____

Now, multiply that number by the number of years you've been drinking or using and write the amount below.

$ _____ x (_____) = $ _____
number of years

➤ Have you ever been fined by the courts for alcohol or drug use? If so, how much? Add up the fines for all of your offenses.

$ _____

➤ How much have you paid for your legal expenses?

$ _____

➤ List all the items you have lost, destroyed, damaged, or pawned as a result of your alcohol or drug use. Estimate the value of these items. If necessary, complete this exercise in a notebook.

Item   Value

_____   _____

_____   _____

_____   _____

_____   _____

_____   _____

_____   _____

_____   _____

_____   _____

Total amount lost: $_____

➤ How much money and how many personal items do you have now? A car? A stereo? A house? Clothes? Jewelry? List them below.

_____   _____

_____   _____

_____   _____

_____   _____

_____   _____

➤ What have you lost? What was seized because of drug sales? List below.

_____   _____

_____   _____

_____   _____

_____   _____

_____   _____

_____   _____

_____   _____

Consider the other effects your use of alcohol or other drugs may have had on your financial condition:

- overspending
- bad or nonexistent credit
- no savings
- loss of job or job promotions
- mismanagement of household funds
- loss of personal goods (such as stereo, car, TV, VCR, etc.)
- kicked out of an apartment for not paying rent
- telephone or electricity shut off

➤ List other examples of how your alcohol or other drug use affected you economically.

_____

_____

_____

_____

➤ How much money could you have earned, but didn't, because of your drug use? Use $8 an hour as a low estimate of your hourly wage. For example, if you hadn't been using, you could have worked 40 hours a week for $8 per hour. Multiply this by 52 weeks. This equals $16,640. Multiplied by ten years it is $166,400. Your counselor should be able to help you with these calculations.

$ _____ x (_____) = $ _____
   hourly wage   hours worked   weekly paycheck
                       per week

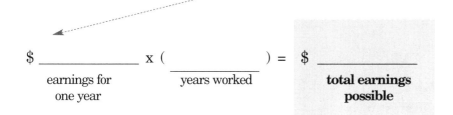

$ _____ x 52 weeks = $ _____
   weekly paycheck   earnings for one year

$ _____ x (_____) = $ _____
   earnings for   years worked   **total earnings**
   one year   **possible**

How much has the community paid for your hearings, trials, and now your incarceration? If you have trouble calculating this, ask your counselor for help.

(Calculate the hourly rate for lawyers at $250 per hour and the cost of daycare at $40 per day per child.)

➤ How much have you cost the state for the following:

- the lawyers who were assigned to defend you

    $ _____

- the prosecutors who prosecuted your case

    $ _____

- the judge who heard your case

    $ _____

- the expense to keep you locked up behind bars

    $ _____

- state and county payments to take care of your kids because you can't do it

    $ _____

Total cost of incarceration $ _____

Job or Profession

Alcohol and other drug use has serious effects on your employment and your ability to get a job.

EXERCISE **19** EXERCISE

Effects of Your Drinking or Using on Your Job or Profession

➤ Did you consider dealing and other criminal behavior to be your "profession"? (check one)

_____ Yes   _____ No

➤ What effects did drinking or using have on your work? (Examples: being fired, having no motivation to look for a job, being absent or late regularly, doing a poor job, and being forced to change jobs.)

_____

_____

➤ Have you ever had a straight job? (check one)

_____ Yes   _____ No

➤ What kinds of jobs did you have when you were not incarcerated?

_____

_____

_____

➤ What was your main source of income when you were drinking and using?

_____

_____

➤ Have you ever had an employer talk with you about your drinking or drug use? What were your employer's concerns?

_____

_____

➤ How has your alcohol or other drug use affected your work and career?

_____

_____

Education

When you were a student, your alcohol and drug use affected your education. Perhaps you

- didn't do homework
- dropped classes
- didn't pay attention in class while high
- were absent often
- dropped out of sports
- had low or failing grades
- missed chance for sports scholarship
- were kicked out of school
- used alcohol or other drugs in school
- isolated yourself from others
- didn't like being told what to do by teachers
- felt out of place in school

 EXERCISE 20 EXERCISE

Effects of Your Drinking or Using on Your Education

➤ List examples of how your alcohol or other drug use affected your education.

_____

_____

_____

_____

_____

Emotional Problems

Because drugs affect your brain, using affects your emotions, too. Different types of drugs cause different emotions. Since alcohol is a depressant, drinking often causes low moods and emotions. High or excited feelings are the result of stimulants like cocaine and meth. Regular use of chemicals can interfere with the normal working of the brain and emotions.

EXERCISE **21** EXERCISE

Effects of Your Drinking or Using on Your Emotional Well-Being

➤ What feelings do you experience when you use your drug of choice?

_____

_____

➤ Are your emotions and reactions more or less intense when you use? Explain.

_____

_____

➤ Are they different now that you're clean? If so, how? Explain.

_____

_____

➤ How often have you told yourself or someone else that you "need" a drink, some pot, or another drug? What were you feeling when you said this? Explain.

_____

_____

➤ People use chemicals to deal with uncomfortable feelings. What feelings did you try to manage with your drug use? Fear? Loneliness? Anger? Rejection? Not being good enough?

_____

_____

➤ How did your alcohol or other drug use increase when you were stressed out? Explain.

_____

_____

Consider how your use of alcohol or other drugs may have affected you emotionally:

- feelings of hopelessness and despair
- emotionally dead—having no feelings at all (except, maybe, anger or self-pity)
- difficulty in getting close to others or expressing feelings
- extreme feelings of loneliness and isolation
- unexplained fears

- thoughts of (or attempted) suicide

- violent thoughts or feelings

- feeling like you had two different lives— one public and one secret

- depression, paranoia, or fear of going insane

- loss of self-esteem

- acting against your own values and beliefs

- strong feelings of guilt and shame

- emotional exhaustion

➤ List examples of how your alcohol or drug use affected you emotionally.

1. _____

_____

2. _____

_____

3. _____

_____

4. _____

_____

Family Problems

Addiction affects families. Family members are the primary target of the addict's abuse or neglect. Often family members don't talk to each other. Feelings are intense. There's often a lot of anger. All the relationships in the family suffer. Consider how your behaviors have interfered with the relationships that mean the most to you. Poor communication with family, living a secret life, stealing from your family, lying, and manipulating are examples.

EXERCISE 22 EXERCISE

Effects of Your Drinking or Using on Your Family

➤ List all the people in your family who have been affected by your alcohol or other drug use and *how* they were affected. Remember, your use affects their body, mind, spirit, job or career, finances, and freedom. If necessary, complete this exercise in a notebook.

Person: _____

Effects: _____

_____

_____

Person: _____

Effects: _____

_____

_____

Person: _____

Effects: _____

_____

_____

Person: _____

Effects: _____

_____

_____

EXERCISE **23** EXERCISE

Effects of Your Drinking or Using on Family Relationships

Your relationships with family members can be affected by your drug use through your behavior. This may include your

- violence—physical, verbal, emotional abuse

- using family members emotionally or financially

- extreme feelings of remorse or guilt

- avoiding or withdrawing from family activities

- missing important appointments (getting kids from school, doctor, dentist, parole officer, etc.)

- increasing marriage or relationship problems

- being unfaithful to your partner or spouse

- infecting your partner with a sexually transmitted disease

- divorce or breakup with partner

- putting your family in danger

- prostitution/pimping

- welfare fraud

➤ List examples of how your alcohol or drug use affected your family relationships. How did you communicate with your family while drunk or high?

1. _____

_____

2. _____

_____

3. _____

_____

4. _____

_____

5. _____

_____

Today, practice taking one step toward something better.

➤ How have you manipulated family members so you could use alcohol or drugs and not deal with the consequences of it? What kind of relationship do you have with these people now?

Person manipulated: _____

What did you do? _____

_____

How was this family member affected? _____

_____

Person manipulated: _____

What did you do? _____

_____

How was this family member affected? _____

_____

Person manipulated: _____

What did you do? _____

_____

How was this family member affected? _____

_____

_____

EXERCISE **23**

➤ If you were living in a home with children, how has your alcohol or other drug use affected them?

_____

_____

➤ If you don't have children, what kind of brother, son, or uncle have you been and how has your alcohol or other drug use affected these relatives?

_____

_____

➤ If you are a father, what kind of father have you been for your kids? How did you neglect them because of your drug use?

_____

_____

➤ How did you involve them in drug selling or drug use? (For example, you made deals from home, they were in the car with you when you were making deals.)

_____

_____

_____

➤ If you are a father, are you proud of the kind of father you have been? If not, why?

_____

_____

_____

➤ List words that best describe the kind of person you are. Include both positive and negative words.

_____ _____

_____ _____

_____ _____

_____ _____

_____ _____

➤ Look at each of the words you listed above. Which ones also describe your father or mother? How are you like your father and mother?

_____

_____

_____

_____

_____

Social Life

Using alcohol and other drugs affects other relationships besides those with your family. Common problems include broken relationships, physical and emotional abuse, neglect, and playing mind games.

What Is a Friend to You?

➤ Describe below what a friend means to you.

_____

_____

_____

_____

_____

_____

_____

Effects of Your Drinking or Using on Your Friends

In what ways have your important relationships with people other than your family been affected by your use of alcohol or other drugs?

Have you

- treated friends badly or lost important friends

- lost interest in hobbies or activities

- lost friends because they didn't approve of your drinking and using behavior

- become isolated from friends

- spent so much time using and dealing that you are not a part of any social activities

➤ Explain your losses in the space below. (If necessary, complete this exercise in a notebook.)

_____

_____

_____

_____

_____

_____

_____

Spiritual Problems

Spirituality involves how we relate to the world around us. Also called your spirit center, spirituality is about how we see the world and all that's in it, and how we see our place in the world.

Your alcohol or drug use has affected you spiritually, perhaps in the following ways:

- by having no spiritual direction
- by sensing that your life has no meaning or purpose
- experiencing a feeling of emptiness
- being lonely and unconnected to anyone or anything
- moving from belief to nonbelief as addiction progresses
- becoming upset or hostile toward any reference to religion or religious beliefs
- staying away from religious activities because of guilt
- violating your morals and values—your sense of right and wrong
- declining morals and values—what wasn't acceptable now is
- feeling abandoned by or angry with God or your higher power
- experiencing a loss of faith in anything spiritual

EXERCISE **26** EXERCISE

Effects of Your Drinking or Using on Your Spiritual Life

➤ How has your alcohol or drug use affected you spiritually?

_____

_____

_____

_____

_____

_____

Legal Problems

You're incarcerated. It's not hard to see that there is a link between your lifestyle of drinking and using and your criminal behavior.

Legal Problems Related to Your Drinking or Using

➤ How was your alcohol or drug use related to your crime? Explain.

_____

_____

_____

_____

_____

➤ List the crimes you committed that involved alcohol or other drug use. What were the consequences of each?

Crime:_____

Consequences: _____

_____

Crime:_____

Consequences: _____

_____

Crime:_____

Consequences: _____

_____

➤ Make a list of the criminal behaviors for which you have not been caught that involved your chemical use.

_____

_____

_____

_____

_____

Note: State and federal law prohibits counselors and other treatment staff from sharing confidential information from a program such as this. However, for your own protection and that of the staff, please speak only generally about your crimes. If you do not list times, dates, or names, you will not incriminate yourself. Talk with your group leader or counselor about the limits of confidentiality.

Community and Culture

The effects of your drinking and using go beyond family and friends. You live in a larger community. Your actions affect your community's schools and churches, neighborhood, culture, and even society as a whole.

Effects of Your Drinking or Using on Your Community and Culture

➤ How have your drinking and other drug-using behaviors affected your local schools? Do they spend extra money on security and try to prevent dealing on and near school grounds?

_____

_____

_____

_____

➤ How have your drinking and use of other drugs affected members of the community churches? For example, have religious communities in your area been forced to take on care of children who aren't being cared for by their addicted parents? Do neighbors feel unsafe in their own homes or out in their yards because of drug-dealing gangs shooting each other up?

_____

_____

_____

_____

_____

➤ How have your drinking and use of other drugs affected your local government? For example, taxpayers pay higher taxes for more police protection, school support, and domestic abuse programs.

_____

_____

_____

➤ How have your drinking and use of other drugs affected society as a whole? For example, taxpayers pay a high price to keep you off the streets and behind bars. Property values are lowered because of crime. Because of theft, department stores raise prices to stay in business.

_____

_____

_____

Consequences of Your Criminal Behavior

There is a connection between your drug use and your addictive and criminal thinking patterns. Studies have shown that the decision to commit most crimes occurs within ten minutes of the criminal act itself.

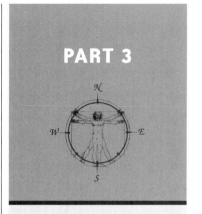

PART 3

A NEW DIRECTION

A Cognitive-Behavioral Treatment Curriculum

Even though you may have had thoughts about committing a crime for days, weeks, months, or even years, you didn't act on them.

Most of the time, the decision to act on those passive thoughts is made on the spur of the moment.

What allows the criminal to have passive thoughts of crime and then suddenly act are types of thoughts called *criminal thinking patterns*. Some examples are the fear of exposure, a lack-of-time perspective, and selective effort. You may have learned about these criminal and addictive thinking patterns in the Criminal and Addictive Thinking module. It would be very useful for you to review that workbook now before going on.

You have just looked at the impact of your drinking and use of other drugs—and you've seen how you have been powerless to stop it. In the following exercises, you'll look at the impact of your criminal behavior on you, your family, and your community.

Miguel's Story (continued)

I used to act like I knew what life was all about, but all in all, I didn't know anything. I'm not trying to act phony, 'cause that's not me. I'm starting to see now that getting into this program has given me a second chance in life. Maybe I won't die on the streets or in prison after all.

— Miguel, incarcerated
A New Direction program participant

Your Crimes

➤ Think about times you committed crimes. What are the exact feelings you got from committing each crime?

1. Crime: _____

   Feeling when committing the crime: _____

   _____

   High during the crime? _____ Yes _____ No

   If high, why? _____

2. Crime: _____

   Feeling when committing the crime: _____

   _____

   High during the crime? _____ Yes _____ No

   If high, why? _____

3. Crime: _____

   Feeling when committing the crime: _____

   _____

   High during the crime? _____ Yes _____ No

   If high, why? _____

4. Crime: _____

   Feeling when committing the crime: _____

   _____

   High during the crime? _____ Yes _____ No

   If high, why? _____

➤ What were the circumstances leading up to and surrounding your current offense and arrest? In other words, what led up to your telling yourself it was okay to commit a crime? An argument? A breakup? A gang issue? A way to get attention? Explain in detail.

   _____

   _____

   _____

   _____

   _____

➤ Who are the victims in your current offense?

   _____

   _____

   _____

   _____

➤ How do you think each of your victims feel about this event?

_____

_____

_____

➤ How were the victims of your crime hurt by it? What happened to them?

_____

_____

_____

_____

_____

➤ Describe what happened the first time you got caught committing a crime. How did you feel?

_____

_____

_____

_____

_____

Powerlessness

➤ Give an example of a time you were preoccupied with a crime you intended to commit. Did that obsession get in the way of other activities in your life? If so, how?

_____

_____

_____

➤ Give an example of a time when you told yourself that you were going to change your criminal lifestyle and then found out that changes were more difficult than you had thought. Explain how you felt. (Powerlessness.)

_____

_____

_____

_____

➤ What are the most common excuses you've used for your criminal behavior?

_____

_____

_____

_____

➤ How did you blame your criminal behavior on someone else?

_____

_____

_____

➤ What thoughts and activities are you preoccupied with now while you are incarcerated? For example, the gym, exercise, using the phones, a TV show, what's happening "on the outside" with friends or family.

_____

_____

_____

What thoughts and activities are you preoccupied with now while you are incarcerated?

EXERCISE **31** EXERCISE

Drugs and Crime

➤ When and how did you use alcohol or other drugs to ease your feelings before, during, or after your crimes? Explain.

_____

_____

_____

Effects of Your Criminal Behavior
on Your Family

➤ List the people in your family who have been affected by your criminal behavior and lifestyle. Describe how your behavior related to your crimes has affected each of these relationships.

Person: _____

Effects: _____

_____

_____

_____

Person: _____

Effects: _____

_____

_____

_____

Person: _____

Effects: _____

_____

_____

_____

Person: _____

Effects: _____

_____

_____

_____

Person: _____

Effects: _____

_____

_____

_____

➤ What has your spouse or partner said to you about your criminal behavior? How did this person cover for you? How is this person still covering for you?

_____

_____

_____

_____

_____

➤ What effect has your criminal lifestyle had on your partner? How do you feel about this?

_____

_____

_____

_____

➤ If you have children, how has your choice to do crime interfered with your relationship with them? How much time with them have you lost because of your criminal behavior?

_____

_____

_____

_____

➤ If you have children, what would you feel and think as a parent if your kids made some of the same lifestyle choices as you?

_____

_____

_____

_____

➤ What do *you* think of your criminal lifestyle? Explain.

_____

_____

_____

➤ How has your criminal behavior and its consequences
interfered with meeting your family obligations? Explain.

_____

_____

_____

➤ What do you think about this?

_____

_____

_____

➤ How do you feel about this?

_____

_____

_____

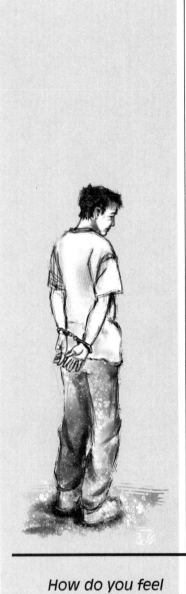

How do you feel when a family member comes to visit you while you're serving time?

➤ What does your family or partner think about you being incarcerated?

_____

_____

_____

➤ How do you feel when a family member (for example, your grandmother, mother, or child) or partner comes to visit you while you're serving time?

_____

_____

_____

➤ How often have you taken something from family members or significant others after they said no or without their knowledge? Why did you do it? Did you believe it was owed to you? Explain.

_____

_____

_____

_____

_____

Effects of Your Criminal Behavior
on Your Friends

➤ What friendships have you lost because of your criminal
behavior? Explain.

_____

_____

➤ How often have you taken something from friends after
they said no or without their knowledge? How did it affect
those relationships?

_____

_____

Effects of Your Criminal Behavior
on Your Jobs

➤ How many jobs have you lost because of your criminal
behavior and its related consequences? Explain.

_____

_____

_____

➤ How many jobs have you just quit because of your distorted thinking? For example, believing the boss was insulting you, that you were "above" doing the kind of work they asked you to do, wanting to start in a job "at the top." Explain.

_____

_____

_____

_____

EXERCISE **35** EXERCISE

More Consequences of Your Criminal Behavior

➤ In what ways did you "profit" by living a criminal lifestyle?

_____

_____

_____

➤ In what ways did you and those around you suffer by your destructive living?

_____

_____

_____

➤ List ten things you have lost due to your destructive lifestyle.

1. _____   6. _____

2. _____   7. _____

3. _____   8. _____

4. _____   9. _____

5. _____   10. _____

➤ What has been the most consistent consequence of your criminal lifestyle?

_____

_____

_____

➤ List three times when your dishonesty caused problems in your life.

1. _____

_____

2. _____

_____

3. _____

_____

➤ List three times when your intolerance caused problems in your life.

1. _____

_____

2. _____

_____

3. _____

_____

➤ List three times when your disrespect caused problems in your life.

1. _____

_____

2. _____

_____

3. _____

_____

Value

➤ What did you value most during your using days?

_____

_____

➤ What are the things you value most now? Does your behavior show this?

_____

_____

➤ What upsets you most about giving up your criminal lifestyle?

_____

_____

➤ What do you think would happen if you started living a productive, responsible life?

_____

_____

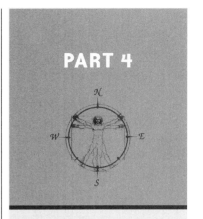

PART 4

Addictive Thinking Patterns

*Addiction is a **thinking** problem before it becomes a **drinking** (or using) problem.*

As an addict, you like to believe that your thoughts and feelings are "special." It's a way to see yourself as unique, valuable, and important. And you have your own "special ways" of doing things.

But no matter what the differences between you and other addicts, all addicts struggle with confused thinking, out-of-control behavior, and the problems that result. The results are very similar to criminal thinking and criminal behavior.

Figure 2 shows how similar the drug and criminal lifestyles are.

Figure 2

THE SIMILARITIES BETWEEN THE DRUG AND CRIMINAL LIFESTYLES

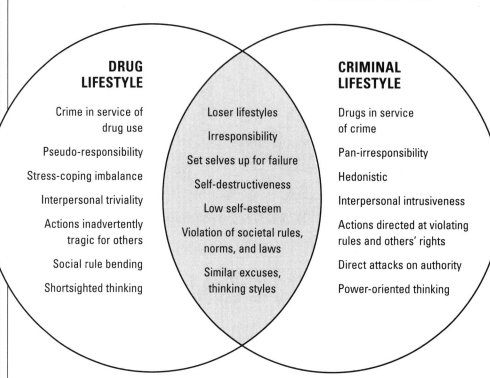

DRUG LIFESTYLE		CRIMINAL LIFESTYLE
Crime in service of drug use	Loser lifestyles	Drugs in service of crime
Pseudo-responsibility	Irresponsibility	Pan-irresponsibility
Stress-coping imbalance	Set selves up for failure	Hedonistic
Interpersonal triviality	Self-destructiveness	Interpersonal intrusiveness
Actions inadvertently tragic for others	Low self-esteem	Actions directed at violating rules and others' rights
Social rule bending	Violation of societal rules, norms, and laws	Direct attacks on authority
Shortsighted thinking	Similar excuses, thinking styles	Power-oriented thinking

Self-Obsession

As an addict, you are pleasure-centered and self-centered. This means your thoughts are controlled by whether or not you feel good. If you don't feel good, you become pre-occupied with what you can do to make yourself feel good again as soon as possible. Because you had a powerful pleasure experience with drugs or alcohol when you first used, your mind became obsessed with repeating that experience. When you feel bad, all you can think about is how to get drugs or alcohol so you will feel like you felt that first time you got high.

You tend to think only about your own wants and needs. Only after your wants and needs are met (for the moment, at least) can you consider the wants and needs of others.

Irrational Thinking

Adding to the problem of self-obsession is another problem called **irrational thinking.** Because your thinking is driven by the obsession to feel good, it becomes irrational. Irrational thinking is insane thinking. It simply doesn't make sense because it is so confusing.

As an addict, you often use irrational thinking because you are not looking for the truth. You are only looking to justify and excuse your single-minded search for getting high. That is why your logic usually goes around in circles, even when it may seem to make sense on the surface.

Your first weapon in the fight against addiction is discovering that addictive thoughts and actions are easy to predict! No matter what the addiction is, all addicts follow a similar pattern. By growing more aware of these patterns, you can watch yourself and others dancing the same tired steps over and over and over again.

> ### Irrational Thinking
>
> *Irrational thinking* doesn't fit with the facts. It contradicts itself. It is confused and disorderly—even insane. It does not use reason to find the truth. It creates arguments to try to prove a lie.

Denial—and How It Keeps You Stuck in Your Addiction

Another huge—and deadly—part of addictive thinking is **denial.** Denial for the addict and alcoholic is the mental ability to deny obvious facts, to turn the truth inside out, to look directly at *down* and believe, with all your heart and mind, that you are really looking *up*.

Denial is not a river in Egypt.

You have just spent a lot of time discovering and looking at the consequences of your alcohol and drug use. You probably had no idea that your use had caused so many problems for so many people—and for you, too. That's denial at work! Some part of your mind just blocked out all that stuff so you didn't have to think about it—and so you could go on drinking and using.

When out-of-control alcohol or drug use is involved, denial becomes a powerful way to protect yourself from discovery—and from help.

With denial, you can see in others what you can't see in yourself. So, you can say something like, "Poor Pete. What a fool. He keeps drinking until he passes out, gets beat up, and robbed. What a chump." You can clearly see how pathetic Pete's situation is. What you can't see is how pathetic your own situation is. Chances are your drinking or using has caused you to be incarcerated, and maybe more than once.

Your mind has dreamed up all kinds of excuses for your use of alcohol or other drugs. Do any of the following sound familiar?

- I only got drunk once in a while.

- No one was hurt.

- Everyone else does it.

- I needed to get my needs met somewhere.

- I can quit when I want to.

- I'm an adult. I can do what I want.

- My situation is different.

Denial

> *Denial* is the unconscious mental strategy used by addicts and alcoholics to keep themselves unaware of the harmful consequences of their use. To deny something is to say it is not true, that it hasn't happened. Though addicts and alcoholics often lie to get what they want, denial is not about lying. Their minds are playing a trick on them. Their minds are making excuses for their use of drugs or alcohol, no matter what harm it does to them or others.

You haven't been able to see the truth about your own drug or alcohol use because of your denial. To see that truth, you'd have to stop drinking or using. And that is what your addictive thinking denies—anything that would suggest you need to stop drinking or using. You *did* begin, however, to see the truth about your life when you started looking at the consequences of your drinking and use of other drugs.

Looking at Denial

➤ Think about ways you've used denial in your life. In the space below, list the reasons you believed—or maybe still believe—that you don't belong in this group for your drug use and criminal behavior. If necessary, complete this exercise in a notebook.

1. _____

   _____

2. _____

   _____

3. _____

   _____

4. _____

   _____

"During my addiction, I pointed the finger of blame at many people and things: my parents, my friends, my past, my environment. Every time I hit my wife, I blamed it on my dad because he hit my mom. Every time I got drunk, I blamed it on my mom because she was an alcoholic. Every time I got into trouble, I blamed it on my friends. Every time I went to prison, I blamed it on my environment. Eventually, I saw that all I had was a whole bunch of finger-pointing.

"The fact of the matter is, I'm an alcoholic and I'm the one in prison. No matter who I blame, I'm the one who has to live with that. So I came to a conclusion. I can keep pointing my finger at other people and remain an alcoholic and keep coming to prison, or I can walk up to the mirror and point the finger at myself. As soon as I did that, I took the first step toward recovery."

— Johnny E.,
   second-degree assault, 3 years,
   Branchville Training Center,
   Indiana
   (Free at Last)

Addictive Thinking Patterns

Addictive thinking patterns are very similar to criminal thinking patterns. Criminal thinking patterns are the types of thoughts that say it is okay to violate others or their property. Addictive thinking patterns justify your use of alcohol and other drugs.

__Addictive thinking patterns__ are ways of thinking that say it is okay to use as much drugs and alcohol as you want, as often as you want, and to do whatever you need to do to get them.

Addictive thinking categories include thoughts that suggest, justify, or promote getting drunk and high no matter what the consequences to yourself or others.

Here are the addictive thinking patterns we've identified:

- self-pity stance
- "good person" stance
- "unique person" stance
- fear of exposure
- lack-of-time perspective
- selective effort
- use of deceit to control
- seek pleasure first
- ownership stance

Your Use of Addictive Thinking

In the spaces below, write how you have used the following addictive thinking patterns to excuse your use of alcohol or other drugs.

➤ **Self-pity stance**
You think the world is out to get you, that you're just a victim of bad luck. You have a hard time taking responsibility for what happens to you. You see yourself as the victim.

EXAMPLES: *"My dad was a drunk and my mom shot heroin. It's not my fault I use."*

"When I was in school, I always got punished for stuff I didn't do. Life's always been unfair to me."

1. _____

_____

2. _____

_____

➤ **"Good person" stance**
Despite all the things you've messed up and all the times you've let yourself and other people down, you still think you're a decent person.

EXAMPLES: *You try to make yourself look good by continually pointing out that someone else is worse than you. You say, "At least I'm not a crack head," or "I'm no gutter drunk like that guy."*

1. _____

_____

2. _____

_____

➤ **"Unique person" stance**

You like to see yourself as different and special. You also tend to romanticize yourself. You may see yourself as a mysterious, adventurous, or tragic figure, like a pirate or an old west cowboy or a gangster or some other super-bad, super-tough character.

EXAMPLES: *"I can drink anybody under the table."*

"Crack takes me places you can't even dream of."

"I've smuggled more junk without getting caught than you'll ever see in your lifetime."

1. _____

_____

2. _____

_____

➤ **Fear of exposure**

You fear you'll be exposed as an addict or alcoholic and
will have to stop using. So you hide your use or you flaunt
it. Either way, you are afraid of changing your life in ways
that might mean changing your use.

EXAMPLES: *You hide how much you drink so others
won't know about your use and challenge
it. Or you take pride in how often you get
high as a power move to make it seem
like nothing can hurt you.*

1. _____

   _____

2. _____

   _____

➤ **Lack-of-time perspective**

Because getting high is the most important thing in your
life, you tend to live only in the present when you are high
and only in the near future ("How can I get more soon?")
when you are not high.

EXAMPLE: *"The future is a long way off. I'm going to
enjoy today by getting high."*

1. _____

   _____

2. _____

   _____

➤ **Selective effort**

You have the energy to fulfill your own pleasure desires, but not enough energy for others, including your children or other loved ones. You have the drive to score and use chemicals, but not to find and keep a job or finish school.

EXAMPLES: *"Hey, somehow things will work even if I don't show up for work tonight. I need a night out."*

"I'm too busy to go to group tonight."

1. _____

_____

2. _____

_____

➤ **Use of deceit to control**

You will lie, cheat, steal, tell half-truths, and beg to get and continue using alcohol or other drugs.

EXAMPLES: *"I told my wife I spent the money on a parking ticket so she wouldn't know I was buying crack."*

"I told my boss I was sick instead of hungover."

1. _____

_____

2. _____

_____

➤ **Seek pleasure first**

You seek the pleasure of getting high without regard for the serious physical, mental, and legal consequences that result.

EXAMPLES: *"I don't have a real problem. I just like to drink when I'm stressed."*

"What's wrong with having a good time?"

1. _____

_____

2. _____

_____

➤ **Ownership stance**

Since you will do whatever it takes to feed your addiction, you mistakenly believe it is somehow okay for you to steal and to cheat others to get what you want most: drugs or alcohol.

EXAMPLES: *Stealing money from a family member to buy drugs.*

1. _____

_____

2. _____

_____

The one I always have to watch is me. I always got myself high.

Character Defects

In addition to addictive thinking patterns, all addicts share certain character defects. The following exercise will teach you how to make your own self-assessment. The purpose is to help you see yourself exactly as you are—without excuses, denial, or minimizing. It will help you accept yourself as you are—the first step toward sobriety.

EXERCISE **39** EXERCISE

Self-Assessment of Character Defects

For each character defect listed below, give specific examples of how this defect applies to your life. Your counselor and senior peers can help you if necessary.

➤ **Self-centeredness**

Self-centeredness means being preoccupied with your own needs and wants: "Me first, last, and always, without concern for the needs and welfare of others in my life." This defect will bring up your dependency on alcohol and other drugs.

_____

_____

_____

_____

_____

➤ **Alibis**

Using *alibis* is your habit of excusing your behavior by *blaming others*. It shows your refusal or inability to accept the responsibility and consequences for your own behaviors. This is very destructive denial. By making excuses, you present a false image of yourself to others.

_____

_____

_____

_____

➤ **False pride**

You build up a false self-image through exaggeration, arrogance, and self-deception. It is denial of who and what you really are.

_____

_____

_____

_____

"I came to prison 21 years ago, and since then I've spent only eight months as a free person. I came to prison with an attitude. I resented authority. I hated being told what to do and when to do it.

"Drugs were easily obtained. Using was our way to beat the system and build 'easy time.' Our view was that they could imprison our bodies, but not our minds.

"We were right; we did that by ourselves. We developed a dependency on those drugs that locked our potential inside a psychological prison with a stronger grip than bars and fences could ever hold.

"I may not be fully recovered yet, but I know what I don't want out of life and that's my guide to what can only get better."

— Phillip W.,
 murder, 30 years,
 Nottoway Correctional Center,
 Virginia
 (Free at Last)

➤ **Resentments**

Resentments show your inability to forgive. Hate, envy, and hostility consume you from the inside out. They feed your destructive anger and desire to seek revenge. You destroy your own peace of mind because other people and the world won't be what you think they should be.

List four of your resentments against specific people or society in general.

1. _____

2. _____

3. _____

4. _____

You will never be able to accept yourself until you can accept others for who they are.

➤ **Intolerance**

Intolerance is your refusal to accept other human beings, beliefs, values, habits, practices, or even conditions of life that are different from yours. It is your inability to accept the mistakes of others. You will never be able to accept yourself until you can accept others for who they are.

_____

_____

_____

_____

_____

➤ Impatience

You have difficulty with any delays on your time, interests, needs, or wants. You are impatient with pain, interruptions, and even your own impatience. This shows your lack of involvement with other people and your self-centered concern only for yourself.

_____

_____

_____

_____

➤ Envy and jealousy

Envy and _jealousy_ involve self-centered preoccupation with another person's abilities, well-being, or good luck. Nothing is good enough for you. This means you are preoccupied with wishful thinking and the big "if only." Nothing can please you because you cannot please yourself.

_____

_____

_____

_____

"I was doing meth a lot, and once I was strung out on meth for like a week. I knew I was high, but I was telling myself that I still had it together. I was having people at my house, but I told myself that at least I was keeping things there together. After I got straight, I could finally see what had really been happening. My house was totally, and I mean TOTALLY trashed. It was a dump. Broken windows, tore up everywhere. And me? Well, I'd been using so much that all the enamel on my teeth was destroyed—I lost all of them now."

— Sean,
   dealing drugs, 10 years,
   Graham Correctional Center,
   Illinois
   (Free at Last)

➤ **Procrastination**

Procrastinators refuse to be responsible—for whatever reason. They put off and postpone things, no matter who suffers. For example, how long have you put off facing the reality of your own addiction?

_____

_____

_____

_____

➤ **Feelings easily hurt**

You have an inner tenderness to life, persons, circumstances, and events. Being self-centered makes life uncomfortable for you and everyone around you. You have an angry need to get even and to punish others for small things. This is a belief and demand that you be treated in a God-like way.

_____

_____

_____

_____

Be kind to your enemies. It will drive them crazy.

➤ **Self-pity**

Self-pity is a totally unmanageable feeling that nobody loves you, life is against you, and God couldn't care less. Feeling this way shows your lack of interest, care, or involvement. You refuse to participate in real life. You believe that the world owes you a living. Your attitude is that you are not good enough. You quit on life, yourself, others, and on anything outside yourself. Addicts say, "Poor me. Who wouldn't drink or use if they were in my place?"

_____

_____

_____

_____

➤ **Fears, worries, and anxieties**

You have an unreasonable obsession about what might happen tomorrow or sometime in the future. It stops you from being able to deal with the responsibilities and commitments you face today.

_____

_____

_____

_____

A closed mouth gathers no foot.

➤ **Guilt, shame, and remorse**

Feelings of *guilt, shame,* and *remorse* show your unreasonable, irresponsible, and immature behavior. They also show your stubbornness when it comes to changing the course of your life. Guilt is your excuse.

_____

_____

_____

_____

➤ Can you see a pattern in your thinking, attitudes, and behaviors? How has this brought self-hate and the need to alter your mood by depending on alcohol or other drugs? Explain.

_____

_____

_____

_____

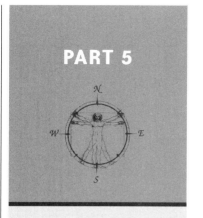

Now Is the Time for Real Change

Addiction is a chronic disease like diabetes or heart disease. You might now be thinking, "Well, I didn't ask for this disease. It's not *my* fault that I've got it, and as long as I do, well, there's not much I can do about it."

Sorry, but that's just not the case.

Your Responsibility

Maybe your parents were addicts and you grew up on the streets. You are still responsible for playing the cards you got dealt. With addiction, just as with other diseases, you have to take responsibility for how you deal with the disease and take care of yourself.

The best medical care in the world won't help someone who isn't willing to follow the treatment for the illness. For you to recover from any disease, you have to take responsibility for yourself. Someone who has diabetes, for example, can't expect to live a long and healthy life without taking insulin and avoiding sweets. Doctors—and chemical dependency counselors—can't magically cure diseases. You need to take responsibility for your health and your actions. As an addict, you need to understand that although you are not responsible for being addicted, *you must be responsible for your own recovery.*

Addiction is not in the bottle or the pill, it's in the person.

You've probably tried to change, control, or stop your addictive and criminal behaviors but weren't successful. That's because you didn't really understand that you had a serious problem. You blamed others for what happened to you. But other people aren't responsible for your actions. Only you are!

Right now, you are probably confused, worried, frustrated, and angry. That's common. It's hard to look at yourself and your past and see all the mistakes you've made.

Now, as you begin to look more closely at the situation you're in and what got you here, you might also feel lost and hopeless. This is normal.

"Resentment is like drinking poison and expecting someone else to die."

— Anonymous

There is good news, although it may be hard to believe right now. The first step in doing something to get better is to understand how big your problem is. You must accept your situation.

You can't begin to fix it until you honestly admit that you have a problem. No more denial. The cards are face up. There's no doubt that you're in a deep hole and can't get out alone.

You have to *fully admit to yourself and fully disclose to others* not only that you have a problem with drugs and crime, but also that you have been powerless to stop and that your life has been unmanageable as a result.

Remember:

Powerlessness is your "out-of-control" behavior— your addiction.

Unmanageability has to do with the consequences of your behavior for you and for others.

Being Honest

This is a very difficult step to take, but it's the foundation of the entire recovery process. It sets the stage for making changes in your life that *cannot* happen unless you recognize the enormous *need* to change.

People don't want to admit defeat, or to change, when they look at themselves and their addictive behaviors. But, as a longtime heroin addict once said, "Help for addicts begins only when we are able to admit complete defeat."

Maybe this seems like a simple idea, but your addiction has made you powerless. It's been the driving force in your life. It doesn't give up easily. That's what denial is all about—finding excuses to continue using and committing crimes.

You have been powerless to control your use. You've been doing drugs against your will. You continue using in spite of negative consequences. Again, you've seen the problems your drug use has brought on. You know you need to stop. You've tried before.

Often, addicts look for a "reason" for the addiction. They want to blame their marriage, job, neighborhood, family, the police, and so on. They'd rather do that than admit that they are the problem. Again, this is just denial at work.

As long as you look for an answer to the problem outside yourself, you won't look at the real problem. Here's the reality, as stated by an addict named Lewis: "Lewis's problem is Lewis." Your addiction problem is your problem, no one else's. You need to surrender, to "admit defeat" to begin recovery. But remember, other people *can* help you recover from your addiction.

You may actually feel defeated. Your outer stance of being strong, powerful, in control, above problems, is crumbling. You may start feeling down about what's happened. This is a positive sign. It means you're getting past your denial.

The Importance of Telling Your Story

Another crucial part of the first step in recovery is to tell addicted others your story. The following story shows the importance of sharing with others.

Some seventy years ago, a stockbroker who was down on his luck because of his drinking problem sat in the kitchen of a house in Akron, Ohio. The house belonged to a doctor who had the same problem. They simply could not stop drinking. They sat over a cup of coffee discussing a letter the broker had received from Carl Jung, a famous physician and pioneer of psychotherapy. In the letter, Jung told them that if their new group was to be successful, they had to pass on their stories. Essentially the key to success was to help each other rather than trying to recover on their own. *Telling of the story* was born and has been the cornerstone of Alcoholics Anonymous (AA). The framework that the founders of this program developed has helped millions— yes, millions—of people recover from many kinds of addiction.

Professionals tried to help for years, but it wasn't until AA came up with the idea of the story that people began recovering from addiction.

Put simply, the story is about change. It's about admitting that you have been powerless over your addiction and that your life has become unmanageable as a result.

 EXERCISE **40** EXERCISE

Telling Your Story

To take your first step in recovery, you need to tell your "story" to your counselor and group. You need to talk about what your life was like, what happened, and what it's like now. Think about all the times you were powerless over drugs, the people your drug use affected, the consequences you've suffered as a result of your use. Be completely honest with yourself and with your group. It's time to tell your story.

People who take this first step usually understand and accept these ideas:

- You must completely accept that you have a problem.

- You recognize there are things happening you cannot control by yourself.

- You have to ask for help from others to be successful in this effort.

- You must focus on what you *can* do.

- You have to give up secrets and stop pretending to be something that you are not.

- Your addiction will continue until you completely accept this lesson—or you will end up behind bars or dead.

Remember, not using is only the beginning of recovery. Once your mind and body are free of alcohol and other drugs, it is finally possible to look at the underlying problems in your life and begin to chart a drug- and crime-free course. Not using is the foundation you must have to begin a program that results in tremendous, positive life changes.

Grief

Once you accept that alcohol and drugs are off limits because you can't control your use, you will begin a grieving process. Chances are you won't even know it's grief. Everyone eventually goes through a grieving process when they finally accept that there are limitations in their lives. There's a feeling of loss when you have to accept that there's an activity—drinking or gambling, for example—that other people can take part in that you cannot. Grief is part of addiction.

Your feelings of grief will likely center around the following four areas:

1. realizing that you can't use alcohol or other drugs anymore

2. the "death" of your addiction and criminal fantasy life

3. the past losses you experienced as a result of your addictive behaviors

4. a fear of not knowing who you'll be or what you will do without these behaviors, because they have been like a "friend" who has provided you comfort for many years

Realizing That You Can't Drink or Use Drugs Anymore

All alcoholics and addicts eventually come to the realization that when they use alcohol and other drugs, they just aren't like most other people they know. Try as they might, they simply can't control their alcohol use. Occasional or moderate use quickly turns into an obsession.

The Death of Your Drug-Related Life

You, like many people, probably had and still have fantasies about your drinking and drug use. You might have felt cool, strong, powerful, important, or respected for your using lifestyle. You thought a "straight" life was boring. But eventually you became so wrapped up in those fantasies that you lost touch with the real world—and became incarcerated. By living in that fantasy world, you prevented yourself from being a person who truly is strong, important, and respected, someone whose life helps others and contributes to society. Your old life has to die before you can create your new life. You have to see yourself as someone who does not drink or use.

Fear of Change: Not Knowing Who You'll Be without Drugs

Over time, your whole identity became wrapped up in your drug use. It became your life focus. In a sense, it defined who you are as a person. You grew comfortable in this identity. Drugs became your best friend. Now, when you're anxious or upset, they are still your source of comfort. Without them, you feel lost. Maybe you don't know anyone who doesn't use or anyone who's successfully quit.

You don't know what's going to happen if you quit. And you are probably scared. And if you are, you probably don't want to admit it, even to yourself.

But that's okay. Lots of people feel afraid when they make even small changes. The following "Temporary Beliefs" section has tips about handling this fear. You aren't the first person to feel this way. And you can get past this. You're stronger than you think—it's just that this is a new situation for you. You will need to take some risks in recovery, but they will be small compared with the risks you took in your drinking/drugging and criminal lifestyle.

You might also feel ashamed. You feel bad about what you're doing, that you're incapable of stopping, and you're worried about how you'll handle life without drugs and crime.

Temporary Beliefs

Change is an important concept in this workbook. We'll help you make positive changes in your life.

Here's the first really important idea to think about:

If you focus only on your behavior, you will be able to make only small changes.

To make a change like you are considering—to quit using drugs and committing crimes—means you have to change your thinking as well as your behavior. You'll need to change the way you see yourself and the world around you. This was one of the most important ideas in the *Criminal & Addictive Thinking* workbooks. You have to change your belief system. You need to stop thinking like an addict and a criminal.

You may not believe that true change is possible for you. Or perhaps you believe you won't be able to do this. So, what *can* you do?

You will need to take on "temporary" beliefs. We are going to suggest some changes to your belief system. Up to now, your view of the world and yourself hasn't worked for you. (If it had, you wouldn't be incarcerated doing drug treatment.) The new beliefs *can* lead you to a better life. You have to trust that these beliefs will work. If you do, eventually, they won't be temporary. They will become your new view of yourself and others. This will help you repair the damage done by your addictive and criminal behaviors.

You will need to do the following:

- Trust the perceptions of others, even if you think they are wrong.

- Trust that you have been damaged far more than you know, but that time and recovery can repair the damage.

- Remember that addiction is a form of insanity that gives you a warped view of others and the world.

- Trust that the only way out of your insanity is to tell those who are helping you all that has happened in your life. They can help you reclaim reality.

- Do not minimize or omit uncomfortable details when telling your story.

- Be completely honest.

- Make a commitment and do not hold back. Anything less than full honesty lowers your chances of success— and increases the odds that one day you'll be right back where you are right now.

- Allow people to care for you, even if you do not feel that you deserve anyone's love or care.

- Follow through on what is asked of you.

- Surrender control of your life to those who can care for you better than you can care for yourself right now.

Remember that addiction is a form of insanity that gives you a warped view of others and the world.

The Critical Importance of a First Step

This first step is not an easy one. It brings emotions to the surface. One of these emotions is fear of the unknown. You may wonder how you can live without drugs. Being worried about this is common. Many other people have felt exactly the same way.

Taking this first step is absolutely necessary. Everything else follows this. Without it, your chances of learning to manage your behavior are slim. This step is the base for all future work. Until you create this foundation, none of the other steps we suggest will work.

Yes, this first step is difficult and painful. But we want to emphasize again that it is the beginning of recovery. Life will feel worse before it feels better because you're eliminating your "medication." The drugs and behaviors you've been using to cover up the pain of all your losses will be gone.

If you look back on your life, do you recall when you started to feel some of the consequences of your behavior? What did you do then? Did you go back to using other drugs? If so, what was the result?

Remember, part of the goal of this first step is to provide a safe place to begin experiencing this pain. It's okay—even necessary—to let yourself experience all the feelings that have been pent up inside you. In the end, you will feel better.

This true story can help you better understand where you're at right now.

When we first begin recovering from addiction, all the thoughts and feelings we've held inside—shame, guilt, remorse, regret—come flooding out, and it's terribly painful for a while. But that pain is a sign that we're still alive. There's hope for us yet because our minds, bodies, and spirit of life haven't given up yet. Sometimes it's best to just admit the pain and even focus on it. It means you're still alive, and the helicopter—your life in recovery—is on the way.

Breaking the Criminal Code

The criminal code. You know it. It's unwritten, but any inmate can talk about it, and most claim to follow it. And you know the consequences for breaking that code. But you must break it before you can get better. It's critical to moving ahead in your recovery. Yes, some people may call you a "treatment loser" if you do, but who's the real loser here?

Case History

A college student was hiking and climbing in the mountains of Colorado. He was on a steep incline when he hit a section of shale that gave way beneath his feet, sending him sliding back down the mountain face, over a cliff, and onto a rock ledge thirty feet below. He landed on his back, his backpack somewhat cushioning the fall, but he broke both legs, several ribs, and crushed two vertebrae. He couldn't move. His climbing partner could not get to him. The partner had to climb all the way back down the mountain and hike several miles to a ranger station to summon help. It took nearly eight hours for the MedEvac helicopter to reach the injured man and airlift him to a hospital.

When asked what he had thought about while he lay helpless on the rock ledge for almost eight hours, the man replied, "I was in excruciating pain, so I just focused on the pain. As long as my body was able to feel all the damage that had been done, I was okay. I knew that when the pain started to leave, that meant my body was giving up and I was going to die. The pain was my proof that I still had a chance."

If you follow the plan in this workbook, you'll have a better chance of staying on the outside if you are released. And while you are incarcerated, you'll be a positive influence for others. If those guys calling you "loser" continue living by the same rules that got them behind bars, they will be back in a cage before they know it. So now who's the loser? You or them?

That's what's really at stake here.

It's your life and your choice.

Stick with a criminal code that's cool in the joint and you'll be cool in the joint. That's where you'll end up living most of your life.

If criminal thinking puts you behind bars and this is where criminals are kept, why hold on to it? The change starts now, and it takes practice. If you wait until you hit the door to practice change, it's too late.

Your only other choice is to live the "responsibility code" (we'll talk about that soon), get out from behind bars for good, and do something with your life that you can be proud of, something that your kids, spouse or partner, parents, and community can be proud of.

Maybe you feel you must be loyal to your friends on the outside who drink and use. Think about it. Are they loyal to you now that you're behind bars? Do they visit you? Send you money? Write to you? Maybe they're only your buddies when you're trying to sell for them or when you're high together. If you continue to hang with your gang, your chances of living past the age of twenty-five aren't very good, either. It's good to be a loyal friend, but you need to decide whether these people deserve your loyalty.

It's time to be loyal to yourself first. You now have a choice to do what is best for you and your children. It's a choice you're going to have to make. It's about the way you think about things and who you choose to hang with. If you think you can be straight and still hang with your old friends, you're only fooling yourself.

What do your old friends do? If they are on the street, they deal, drink and use, and commit crimes. How will you hang with them and not do the same? Ask around. See how many guys thought they could do this . . . and where are they now? It's going to be difficult. Very difficult. Especially at first. But it's possible. Lot's of people have done it. You can, too.

EXERCISE **41** EXERCISE

Your Involvement in the Criminal Code

➤ What are the "rules" of the criminal code—as you see them?

_____

_____

_____

_____

➤ Give three examples of the criminal code you are now using.

1. _____

2. _____

3. _____

➤ Give three examples of how you have used the criminal code in the past week.

1. _____

2. _____

3. _____

➤ How has the criminal code hurt you and the community here in your group?

_____

_____

_____

EXERCISE **42** EXERCISE

Beliefs That Keep You Involved in the Criminal Code

➤ Let's look at beliefs that keep you in the criminal code. Give an example from your life for each one. For example, under item 1, your belief might be "I'm older and smarter than the others."

1. It's my right to be in charge.

_____

_____

2. I need to control what others do, say, think, and feel in order to dominate them.

_____

_____

3. I want to be at the center of things.

_____

_____

4. I keep the control in any way I can.

_____

_____

5. I claim that "I'm the victim" when held accountable.

_____

_____

6. I get excitement from pursuing power.

_____

_____

7. I think of myself as a leader and look for chances to exercise power through leadership.

_____

_____

8. I refuse to be dependent on others unless I can take advantage of them.

_____

_____

9. I can never lose.

_____

_____

10. My self-esteem depends on getting my way with others.

_____

_____

11. I never have to face how ordinary I am.

_____

_____

12. If I ask for help, I am weak.

_____

_____

It's time to be loyal to yourself first.

Consequences of Keeping the Criminal Code

➤ In the space below, list how staying in the criminal code affects people in these areas of your life.

Your family:

_____

_____

_____

Your friends:

_____

_____

_____

Your neighborhood:

_____

_____

_____

Your community:

_____

_____

_____

How Your Keeping the Criminal Code
Affects Others in Your Life

When you live the criminal code, it affects others, too. Below, write the names of people who have been affected by your keeping the criminal code. For example, for the first, name the people you manipulated and intimated to help get you alcohol or other drugs or to cover for your use.

➤ People who feel used, manipulated, lied to, threatened, abused, and intimidated:

_____   _____

_____   _____

_____   _____

➤ People who feel scared:

_____   _____

_____   _____

_____   _____

➤ People who feel insecure, not knowing what will happen next:

_____   _____

_____   _____

_____   _____

▶ People who feel powerless:

_____   _____

_____   _____

_____   _____

"I don't know how to face my
people when they come to visit
me. They try to be nice, but I
know I've let them down."

— Calvin T.,
   aggravated assault,
   4 years,
   Cook County Jail, Illinois
   (Free at Last)

▶ People who feel inferior and stupid because of how you
treated them:

_____   _____

_____   _____

_____   _____

▶ People you treat as though they have no rights so they lose
their own sense of self-worth and self-respect:

_____   _____

_____   _____

_____   _____

▶ People who feel afraid to do anything on their own without
checking with you first:

_____   _____

_____   _____

_____   _____

➤ People who feel lonely, yet are afraid to leave you:

_____

_____

_____

➤ People who think they can't trust anybody because you won't let them:

_____

_____

_____

EXERCISE **45** EXERCISE

Why Do You Keep Holding on to the Criminal Code?

➤ Why do you think you continue to keep the criminal code?

_____

_____

_____

_____

_____

"It's not enough to recover just because it may help you get out of prison sooner. Why get out sooner if you are just going back to the same old life that got you to prison in the first place? You have the time now to better yourself, so do it! I know it's hard, but you can do it. I have faith in you, and that's what you have to have in yourself. Don't let what happened to me happen to you!"

— Feltus T.,
murder, death penalty,
St. Clair Correctional Facility,
Alabama
(Free at Last)

The Responsibility Code

The responsibility code replaces the criminal code. Living this code will literally save your life. The responsibility code states the following:

1.

I will put others first, looking for what is best for them.

2.

I will not feel like the victim if I genuinely
care about others.

3.

I do not put people behind bars; they put themselves
behind bars. Incarceration might *save* their lives.

4.

When I choose not to be alone, I'll join others who
are doing whatever it takes to live responsibly.

5.

I am responsible for what *I know*—I will not run,
hide, or keep it secret, because then I am "using" again.

6.

I will harm others if I know about or see them
hurting themselves and do nothing.

7.

When my motive is to *do whatever it takes* to think
and act responsibly, I will put others first and respect
myself, finding peace, honesty, and joy inside.

8.

Life is not a game of win or lose; we all can win.

What's Holding You Back from Living the Responsibility Code?

➤ What are the most difficult things you must overcome in changing? What makes it hard to do treatment in a correctional facility and to live by the responsibility code?

_____

_____

_____

_____

➤ How did you break the criminal code? What are some things guys who are changing can expect if they break it?

_____

_____

_____

_____

➤ What will you gain by breaking the criminal code?

_____

_____

_____

_____

Following the Responsibility Code

How will your living by the responsibility code affect the following people? For each, give at least five ways their lives will be better when you follow this code.

➤ Your family:

1. _____

2. _____

3. _____

4. _____

5. _____

➤ Your friends:

1. _____

2. _____

3. _____

4. _____

5. _____

➤ Your neighborhood:

1. _____

2. _____

3. _____

4. _____

5. _____

➤ Your community:

1. _____

2. _____

3. _____

4. _____

5. _____

"The truth will set you free. Never having to hold secrets that might involve harming someone. Never worrying about being arrested or shook down. No more pain from committing assaults and hurting other people. Being comfortable with authority. Inner peace from knowing we are doing the right thing. You can't really care about anyone at all and still hold to the criminal code."

— Ricky H.,
criminal negligent homicide,
27 years,
Cook County Jail,
Illinois
(Free at Last)

To Stay or Leave, It's Your Decision

➤ What are your reasons against leaving the criminal code?

_____

_____

_____

➤ What are your reasons for leaving the criminal code?

_____

_____

_____

Behaviors That Follow the Responsibility Code

➤ Look back at the answers you gave in exercise 42. Now, write new, responsible thoughts and behaviors you will practice instead. (If necessary, complete this exercise in a notebook.)

_____

_____

_____

_____

Who Do You Respect? And Why?

Your criminal lifestyle has made you loyal to your friends and your drinking and using buddies. But think for a moment. Who do you *really* look up to? What person do you really respect? Is it a gang leader? Is it someone who's an addict and drug dealer? Probably not. Who are the people you truly respect and what do they do? They have jobs, don't they? Maybe it's your grandmother, a social worker you know, a former schoolteacher, or someone who runs the local community center.

These are people you can see who are making a difference. Okay, maybe they don't drive the best car in the world. But what do they have that you don't? They probably have a family. They are free, not incarcerated. They don't worry about getting shot, about not having a job. And they have the respect of their family and friends and people in their community—respect that they've earned because of who they are and what they do for others and their community.

The people you respect probably live in the same environment you came from, but they are making different choices. And if you ask them, they'll tell you that they like who they are and they're happy with life. And that's probably not something you can say about you and your life right now, is it?

But you can change that.
With time, hard work, and courage,
you can be that kind of person.

Until now, you have been a loyal and responsible criminal. Now you need to be loyal and responsible in a different way for different goals. And this *can* be done.

What Will Other People Think?

One thing you have to stop worrying about is what certain people are going to think. Now and in the past, you have focused on how other people saw you. You look for approval from other people. You worry about your image. For right now, try forgetting that and start thinking about what your children will think of you. Or what your parents will think of you. And most important, what *you* think about yourself and your life.

Miguel's Story (continued)

I never knew what "integrity" really meant. I didn't follow any standard—I just did what I needed to do according to the needs of the moment. Then, in prison, there was the criminal code to follow, and again I did what I "had to." To change, I had to establish and follow a set of values. Something's either right or wrong; there can't be any in between. Having integrity means having and living where right and wrong are clearly different. It's a simple idea, but for a long time, it wasn't easy to establish.

— Miguel, incarcerated
A New Direction program participant

More about Fear

Let's say that you want to get out and get your life together. But while you're incarcerated, fears and emotions can hold you back. You might fear

- being responsible
- breaking the criminal code
- being called a "snitch"
- danger

- being rejected by old friends

- showing vulnerability

- being exposed

- extortion

- life without alcohol and other drugs

- having to make new friends

- being seen as weak

- change

- letting others know you

- being raped

- retaliation against you and your family

EXERCISE **50** EXERCISE

Fears That Keep You from Changing

➤ Have you experienced fears like the ones listed above? You aren't the only one experiencing them. List your three biggest fears and describe how you have been dealing with these fears.

1. _____

_____

2. _____

_____

3. _____

_____

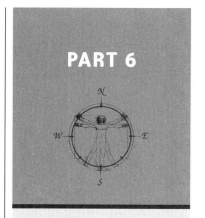

Making Changes

*It's not the size of the step
that matters, just that you take it.*

We've talked before about making changes —about how you need to accept some ideas about this on faith. Now, we'll look at this idea of change more carefully.

You've tried to make changes in your life before. Maybe you did it for a while, but then slowly fell back into your old ways. And maybe you finally gave up because it was too hard to change.

Making changes is hard. Each year, people forget their New Year's resolutions. People promise themselves they will lose weight, quit smoking, or exercise more. You've probably tried to change your drug use or criminal behavior—but you couldn't do it.

Making life changes takes more than a promise to yourself. Although it is difficult, many addicts have quit using. It is possible. That's what this section is about: learning how to change and keep the changes you make.

Six Stages of Change

There are six steps, or stages, of change. Each step is predictable and clear. Everyone goes through them when they make a change. Change doesn't happen all at once. It takes place over time and includes a series of tasks that must be completed. Each stage doesn't have to lead to the next; it is possible to become stuck at one stage or another. By understanding these stages, you can gain control over the cycle of change. You'll move through it more quickly— and with less struggle.

As you read through these stages, keep in mind some changes that you've made—or tried to make—in your life. Try to see how these stages apply to them. At the end of this section, we'll ask you to describe a change you've made, or tried to make, and apply what you did to the steps we're about to describe.

Here are the six stages of change:

Stage 1— Pre-awareness: Before you're even thinking about changing.

At this stage, you're not thinking about changing anything. It's not that you can't see the solution. It's that you don't even see the problem!

Stage 2— Contemplation: Thinking about changing.

Here you have an idea that something is wrong in your life. You kind of see the problem, and you begin to think about what to do.

Stage 3— Preparation: Getting ready to change.

You see the problem and you are planning to take action soon. You want to change and you feel ready to change. But you still have mixed feelings about doing this.

Stage 4— Taking action.

You begin to change your behaviors. You do something—stop smoking, stop drinking, stop using. You take action.

Stage 5— Avoiding relapse.

Don't slip back into negative thinking or behaviors.

Stage 6— Maintenance.

Change doesn't end with the action stage. You have to stay changed. You work to make the change stick. You struggle to prevent lapses and relapse.

Remember: Change will feel uncomfortable. You might think you can just slide right into something new, but it doesn't work that way. You'll feel like there is a tug-of-war inside you about things like breaking the criminal code or

These six stages of change are adapted from the book *Changing for Good,* by James O. Prochaska, John C, Norcross, and Carlo C. DiClemente (New York: Avon Books, 1995).

talking about your feelings. If you're not uncomfortable, you're probably not doing enough. And if you're feeling uncomfortable about this, you're probably doing the right thing. Think back to your early using days. That life wasn't easy either, especially at first.

Stage 1—Pre-awareness: Before You're Even Thinking about Changing

In this stage, it's not that you can't see the solution; it's that you can't even see the problem! You don't want to change anything because you don't think you have any problems in need of change. Although other people in your life—such as your family, friends, neighbors, ministers, or the court system—can see the problem clearly, you can't.

Most people in this stage don't want to change themselves. They want to change the people around them. They often show up in a treatment program because of pressure from others. It might be a partner who threatens to leave them or an employer who threatens to fire them. They may end up behind bars, mandated to go through drug treatment.

Whatever the reason, the push to change comes from someplace or someone else. Their first response in treatment is often, "How can I get everyone to get off my case? How can I get through this?" When all else fails, they may pretend to change, but only as long as there is constant outside pressure. When that's gone, they quickly return to their old ways.

People at this stage resist change. When their problem comes up in conversation, they shift the subject. Denial is typical. They use many excuses to place the blame for their problems on family, their victim(s), society, or whatever. They also tend to feel helpless. They don't want to think, talk, or read about their problems. Because they feel the situation is hopeless, they believe others can't help them, either.

Stage 2—Contemplation: Thinking about Changing

People in the contemplation stage might be thinking, "I want to stop feeling stuck," or "Maybe my counselor *is* right. Maybe I do need to change." They are beginning to think about their problem. In this stage, people admit that they have a problem and begin to think seriously about solving it. They struggle to understand their problem, to see what caused it, and to find solutions. Many think about a plan to take action—not now, however, but "sometime."

In this stage, you are aware that something is wrong in your life. You begin to notice that some "difficulties" have come up—like being incarcerated, for example. You know that these problems are due to your increasing involvement with drugs and crime. You think that maybe what you're doing is a "problem." You think about making some changes, putting some controls on your use, and cutting down a bit. You are more careful about not getting caught the next time. Maybe you even think about getting some help for your using behaviors—but you're not really ready to go to work on yourself yet.

This stage can seem strange. You have an idea of what you want to do, and even how to do it, but you are not quite ready to go. Many people remain in this stage for a long time. Many spend years telling themselves that someday they'll change. But they do nothing about it.

Stage 3—Preparation: Getting Ready to Change

To get to the preparation stage, you already made two changes.

- First, you start to focus on the **solution** rather than the problem.

- Second, you start to think more about the **future** than the past.

Most people in this stage plan to take action soon, often within a few weeks. An important step now is to talk with other people about your goal. Tell your group, your family, and your friends what you are going to do. This will be hard. But you won't ever be free of your addiction until you do. Although in this stage you are committed to acting and seem ready to do it, you will have serious second thoughts. You may still need to convince yourself that the change you are making is what is best. You may already have begun a number of small changes, such as cutting back on your drug use.

People who cut this stage short—for example, waking up one morning and deciding to quit drinking or using cold turkey—actually lower their chances of success. It's better to plan your change carefully and make sure that you have learned what you need to know to carry you through the process.

You might be asking yourself questions like, "Do I need to quit drugs altogether?" "What about my old friends?" "Can I never go to a bar again?" "What do I need to be careful of?" "Can I still deal, but just not use?" "What is it exactly that I need to change?" In other words, what do you need to do to make the change happen?

Worry and fear are often the reason for finally taking action. In your case, maybe you're tired of being behind bars and don't ever want to come back. Maybe you know that another offense will get you more serious time. Maybe you're worried that dealing might get you killed—something you always thought couldn't happen to you. Worry and fear can have a positive effect. They can get you to finally do something to fix your life. Without them, there is often no change. If life is comfortable, why rock the boat?

Stage 4—Taking Action

The action stage involves changing your behavior and surroundings. People in this stage stop smoking cigarettes, get rid of all the potato chips in their house, stop dealing, pour the last beer down the drain, or send all the pornography to the dump. In other words, they make the move they've been planning but have been afraid to make.

For you, taking action would be stopping your criminal activity and use of alcohol and other drugs. You would start to look at the results of your using.

The danger is that you might think "action" is the same as "change." Quitting alcohol or drug use is an action, but "staying quit" is the change. It doesn't mean much to stop for a week or two. You want to stop using forever. That's change.

The action stage is not the only time you can make progress toward overcoming your problem. Although changing your behavior is the most visible form of change, it is not the only one. You can also change your thinking, how you deal with emotions like anger and frustration, and how you see yourself. And many of those changes take place before the action stage. Taking action *is* great progress. But so was simply admitting that you needed to change.

Change is a process, not an event.

Stage 5—Avoiding Relapse

Once you've begun your recovery and started feeling better, you'll need to be careful about slipping back into negative thinking and behaviors. In fact, your thinking will "slip" or "lapse" way before you have an actual relapse.

Examples of thinking slips or lapses include

- undermining your treatment program, by putting it down, for example
- thinking about using
- seeing yourself as a victim
- telling yourself you've been "good" and deserve to use
- glorifying your use

Stage 6—Maintenance

Every stage has its challenges, and the maintenance stage is no different. Here you need to work to prevent lapses and relapses. This stage is very important. It can last from as little as six months to the rest of your life. Without a strong commitment to keeping your change in place, you will relapse.

Preventing Relapse

Making changes is not like flipping a light switch—as in, "I did things this way yesterday," and now (flipping the switch), "I'll do those things differently today." In a way, relapse is a normal part of the change process.

But there's a big, big difference between a relapse for you and relapse for alcoholics who have never been incarcerated. If they relapse, they might miss a day of work or their kid's softball game. But chances are, they won't end up incarcerated for relapsing.

Your situation is very different. You are an addict *and* a criminal. When you relapse and start using again, you will hurt or kill someone. You're like the tornado we talked about at the beginning of this workbook. Your using will build up and you'll quickly find that you're a full-blown tornado. You can't control yourself and you damage or destroy everyone you touch. You'll be right back where you are now, but with even more time to serve.

That's why it's so important to pay attention to your thoughts.

Watch for signs of criminal thinking and addictive thinking. That's when you have to recognize your lapses—*before* you've actually done something that violates your parole, something that hurts someone, something that's illegal.

If you catch yourself slipping in your thinking, you may feel embarrassed, ashamed, and guilty. You may think all of your efforts at change have been wasted. You may want to give up on changing altogether.

After several setbacks, you may feel like you are going in circles. But you're not. Think of the change cycle not as a circle, but as an upward spiral. You may be in the "thinking about" or planning stage again, but this time you can draw on the lessons you learned earlier. You can see what you need to work on more. A lapse is not a failure. You've prepared and taken action before. If you slip up in your thinking, you can keep moving through stages 2 and 3 again. You figure out what you're doing, see how you slipped, and determine what you can do to prevent another. Your goal is to learn from your slip.

This process of change and recovery is a way of living life more fully and being more aware of yourself and your actions. It's not something that you do for a few days, weeks, or months, and then say, "Great! That's done. Time to move on."

Everyone moves through these stages when they make any change in their life. The stages apply to all behaviors.

"If nothing changes, nothing changes."

—Earnie Larsen

Short-Term and Long-Term Change

There are two kinds of change: short-term and long-term.

Short-term changes are very specific steps you can take to stop a problem right now, but they won't help you stop your addiction forever. Short-term changes could mean that you stop hanging with guys who use, stop calling your using friends, or stop telling war stories about your drug use and criminal activities. Short-term changes are a way to stop drinking and using long enough to begin making other changes that will help you stop for the long term.

Long-term changes are the steps you take to change the way you live. Examples of long-term changes include taking part in and completing treatment, getting a sponsor, building new friendships with sober people, and going regularly to support meetings.

Here's another way to think about this. Imagine you have just been shot. When the paramedics arrive, the first thing they do is to see if you're breathing. Then they stop any bleeding that could kill you right away. They will also set any broken bones at this time. Short-term changes are the splints and bandages you need to take care of the obvious and immediate problems. They will save your life in the short run.

If the bullet hits you in the stomach or chest, however, your life is still in danger. Treating only the outside wounds won't save your life. Dealing with internal injuries takes more time and care. You'll need surgery and time in a hospital to completely recover. Repairing these injuries takes more time, but eventually all of you is healed, inside and out.

To heal from addiction, you first need to stop using— and that takes some short-term changes. *Then* you need to heal on the inside. That's when long-term changes come in. Long-term changes involve looking inside yourself to see what's wrong and learning to heal yourself so you don't "need" or want to use anymore.

Making Short-Term Changes

Think about why drug use has been so appealing to you. You might look back at the work you did in exercise 12 to help you understand what attracted you to alcohol, drugs, and criminal behavior. Before you can change your behavior, it's important to be aware of exactly what you like about it.

To heal from addiction, you first need to stop using—and that takes some short-term changes.

The Appeal of Criminal and Addictive Behaviors

➤ What did you like best about using alcohol and other drugs?

_____

_____

_____

➤ What did you like best about your criminal activities?

_____

_____

_____

■

Some crisis related to your addictive or criminal activities got you incarcerated, and something prompted you—or forced you—to seek help for this problem. You know you have to do something to stop these behaviors. This is very common. Crises often force us to make changes in our lives.

The information and exercises in this section are designed to help you immediately stop your addictive and criminal activities. This is a "damage control" mode.

Once you've gotten some control over your drinking and using behaviors, you will be able to see what factors played a role in your addictive and criminal behaviors. You'll be able to deal with these problems and live a better, happier life without drugs or crime.

Past Changes You've Made to Try to Control Using or Criminal Behaviors

➤ Have you tried to stop your addictive or criminal behaviors but failed? Maybe the steps you took were really just short-term changes. In the space below, list three changes you have made in the past to control your addictive and criminal behavior.

1. _____

   _____

2. _____

   _____

3. _____

   _____

➤ What were you hoping to accomplish by attempting these changes?

   _____

   _____

➤ What were the results of your attempts?

   _____

   _____

➤ Were the changes you made short-term?

_____

_____

_____

Making even short-term changes can lead to some very positive feelings.

Looking at your answers from exercise 52, you can see that short-term changes—like getting rid of your drugs, staying away from friends who drink and use, and staying out of bars—are only temporarily effective. Long-term change requires additional steps. You'll need to do more work to make these changes permanent and to recover from your addiction.

Making even short-term changes, however, can lead to some very positive feelings. These feelings are real. You have made a change. You now have a glimpse at what life can be like when you are free of addictive and criminal behaviors. To be chemical-free and crime-free *in the long run,* you need to continue working. At times you may feel worse before you feel healthy again. That's just part of the process. Don't give up. You can do it.

Setbacks are common. When you have one, you may be tempted to say, "See, I failed. I knew there's no point in trying. I'm just going to go get high." Don't take that road. Try not to feel ashamed or feel like a failure. Try to stay calm, and focus on what you have accomplished. Remember the steps to change you just learned about. This is just part of the process of growth and change.

Remember this rule:

**Recovery is about continuing to take steps forward
even if you take some steps backward, too.**

And most important, remember that you *are* doing something positive. You're trying to change and grow. Give
yourself credit for this. You have taken a big and important
step forward.

Summarizing Your Problem Behaviors

To control your addiction, you need to develop relapse
prevention plans. First, however, you need to see exactly
what you have to "prevent." To do this, look at your answers
to exercise 14, Powerlessness Inventory, and answer the
following questions.

➤ What days of the week did you drink or use drugs?

_____

_____

➤ How many hours a day were you using?

_____

_____

➤ What times of day did you typically use?

_____

_____

➤ Where did you typically use?

_____

_____

➤ What excuses did you give yourself for using?

_____

_____

➤ What did you think alcohol and other drugs would do
for you? Give you a high? Reduce stress? Make you not
have to be responsible?

_____

_____

➤ How did you typically feel when you used?

_____

_____

➤ What patterns do you see in your use?

_____

_____

Keep these patterns in mind as you read through the following suggestions for making short-term changes.

The short-term changes you need to make fit into clear categories—reducing access, reducing anonymity, reducing your ownership stance, and making yourself accountable. Short-term changes in each of these categories include the following:

1. **Stop using alcohol and other drugs.**

   - Don't hang out in bars or around liquor stores.

   - Don't hang with your friends when they've gotten together just to get high.

   - Don't hang out with your old gang friends.

2. **Tell others about your commitment to change.**

   - No more hiding behind false identities.

   - No more secrets.

   - Tell a trusted person about your problem.

3. **Drop your "ownership stance."**

   - Work to remember that all the people you come in contact with are *real people* with feelings and families, and so on. They will be hurt if you steal from them, do drugs, ignore them, or break your promises. People aren't just objects for you to use.

4. **Make yourself accountable.**

   - Allow a trusted friend or sponsor, your counselor, or your treatment supervisor to watch your behaviors. Make yourself accountable to this person now during incarceration and later when you are outside.

Six Steps That Can Help You Change

Look closely at the six steps to helping you change on page 183. You'll see that you've already taken some of them. You've become more **aware** of your problems with alcohol and other drugs. You've developed a **desire** to do something about your problems. You've begun changing your **attitude** about your drinking and using and what you need to do in your life. Next, we will help you develop the **skills** you'll need to live a life free of alcohol and other drugs—and free of criminal activity. And that will bring a change—for the better—in your **behavior.**

Finding Others to Support Your Recovery Efforts

As you have discovered, people like you who are addicted can't handle using any amount of alcohol and other drugs.

Help is available to you, even while incarcerated. Take as much action as you can now. Your correctional facility may provide access to Alcoholics Anonymous (AA) or Narcotics Anonymous (NA) prison ministries groups and meetings. You can also find help through other abstinence-based groups like Men for Sobriety, SOS, Amicus, 13 Feathers, and Walking the Red Road.

Remember, you need to find a sponsor, a trusted person you can talk with about your addiction and recovery. AA has programs that allow you to arrange for a sponsor while you're still incarcerated and keep the same sponsor when you are released.

If none of these options are available to you while incarcerated, talk to your group leader or counselor for help in finding a sponsor. Maybe an elder peer who is farther along in recovery than you can be your sponsor. Check with your counselor or group leader to begin making arrangements for a sponsor at least three months before your release date.

Figure 3

Six Steps to Change

NOT AUTOMATIC: Each requires conscious effort	**WANT TO**	**Step 1: AWARENESS** Self-awareness is the first step in changing who you are. You must accept your faults. You can't change who you are without becoming self-aware. **Step 2: DESIRE** If you don't want to change, you won't. You cannot be forced. You have freedom to choose. It is up to you; it is your choice. No desire, no change! **Step 3: ATTITUDE** If you are aware of your faults and want to change, you will automatically improve your attitude. A change in attitude has to come from inside you. It's your choice.
	HOW TO	**Step 4: SKILL** Self-awareness, desire, and a positive attitude are not enough. You must also develop the skills and knowledge of *how to change*. Wanting to change is not enough.
	WHAT TO	**Step 5: BEHAVIOR** Complete steps 1 through 4 and you are ready physically to do what is necessary to change. Do it for ninety days and it will become a habit. Do it for a year and it will become part of you.
AUTOMATIC	**CHANGE**	**Step 6: SUBCONSCIOUS HABIT** Once you get a habit into your subconscious, it becomes automatic. You don't have to think about it anymore. You have changed.

Adapted from a model used by James O. Prochaska, John C. Norcross, and
Carlo C. DiClemente, *Changing for Good* (New York: Avon Books, 1995).

Finding and regularly seeing a therapist after your release, if you can do this, can help you in many ways. Problems with addictive and criminal behaviors are often symptoms of deeper, unresolved, long-term problems such as depression or childhood issues. Dealing with depression or anxiety requires help from a professional. Some people also find that medications help them with these problems.

You may question whether you really need so much help in dealing with these behaviors. Again, it's important to accept that you have a problem. If you'd been able to handle alcohol and other drugs on your own, you wouldn't be incarcerated right now and in this program. Depression, anxiety, and addiction, for example, have nothing to do with willpower or how strong a person you are. You need more help to work through these problems.

We also want to stress the importance of combined therapies. Too often, people seeking help for an addictive behavior will select only one source of help, such as a Twelve Step group, group therapy, or seeing a therapist. This strategy can work, but using a combination increases the chances of your success.

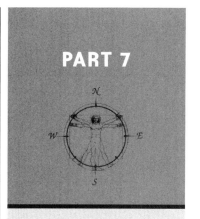

Developing a Relapse Prevention Plan

You've been doing this work long enough to see that recovery takes more time, energy, and emotional involvement than you first thought. Information and exercises in this section can help you recognize when you are in danger of a relapse and learn some ways to prevent it. Preventing relapse requires long-term changes that can help you live a life free of drinking, using, and criminal behaviors.

First, let's look more closely at what leads up to a relapse. Addicts see relapses as a matter of impulse—as a moment of weakness when you let down your guard. *This is not true.*

Stress, coping strategies, and decision-making skills all play a role, as do SUDs (seemingly unimportant decisions). Relapse is the *final* result of a chain of events that starts days, weeks, or even months before it happens. Figure 4 shows how this works.

Figure 4
CRIMINAL BEHAVIOR AND ALCOHOL-OTHER DRUGS RELAPSE CYCLE

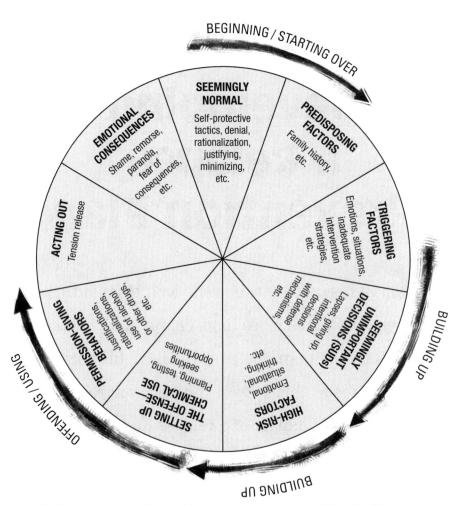

This figure is adapted from *A Structured Approach to Preventing Relapse: A Guide for Sex Offenders,* by Robert E. Freeman-Longo and William D. Pithers (Brandon, Vt.: Safer Society Press, 1992).

People who are headed for a relapse make a number of minor decisions over time, each of which brings them a bit closer to the brink of the triggering high-risk situation.

Often, the actual relapse doesn't happen immediately because the time isn't right. You first relapse "in your mind" by secret planning or fantasies. Then you rationalize those thoughts away or deny having had them, or both. These two distorted ways of thinking come together to create a chain of events leading to a relapse.

People slowly set the stage for a relapse by making a series of seemingly unimportant decisions (SUDs), each moving them another step closer to relapse. For example, a recovering alcoholic who buys a bottle of gin to take home, "just in case guests drop by," is making an SUD. So is a former marijuana user who agrees to "hang on to some weed" for a friend, "just to help him out, not to use."

When you "set up" a relapse like this, it gives you an excuse to avoid responsibility for the relapse. By putting yourself in a very high-risk situation, you can claim you were "overwhelmed" by a situation that made it "impossible" to resist relapse. The reality is that *you* put yourself in a position to be "overwhelmed." You are *always* the one responsible for your behavior.

Don't Underestimate Stress

Stress can be a powerful relapse trigger—one you should never underestimate. Consider this scene: You've recently moved back in with your partner and your son. Over the past few weeks, your son has been having problems at school that have been taking extra time. Some surprise medical expenses are making money tight this month. Also, your partner has been worrying about an upcoming visit from her parents.

As a result, there's a lot more tension around your house than normal. It's been building up for a few weeks, wearing you down. You've been thinking more and more about how great it would be to have a few beers or a joint, just like old times. You've stopped yourself so far, with the help of your sponsor. But now it's Friday night, and you're home alone. You know the local liquor store will deliver and your pot-smoking buddies are just a phone call away.

Lapse vs. Relapse: What Is a Lapse?

A *lapse* happens when you are very close to drinking, doing drugs, or getting involved in criminal activity, but haven't actually "crossed the line." You put yourself in a situation where you've used before and would be tempted to use again. You've made some SUDs that are bringing you close to relapse. For example, a lapse while you are incarcerated would be hanging out with guys you know still use drugs, or trying to find out who's got drugs or who's using, or just thinking about using.

Here are some other examples:

- hanging on the street with friends who are selling drugs, even though you're not actually selling

- telling "war stories" with fellow inmates

- not attending meetings regularly

- cutting back on support group meetings

- thinking you don't need to attend meetings because you're "better" now

- isolating yourself from people who are helping you stay sober

- looking to find faults in staff and other inmates as excuses to use

- looking for negative things about your meetings

A *relapse* happens when you actually use alcohol or drugs or take part in criminal activity.

We want to help you become more aware of your lapse and relapse warning signs—and this exercise can help you do that.

EXERCISE **54** EXERCISE

Lapse and Relapse Warning Signs

➤ What would be a lapse for you? Give three examples.

1. _____

2. _____

3. _____

➤ What would be a relapse for you? Give three examples.

1. _____

2. _____

3. _____

➤ What are five emotional signals that show you may be at risk for a relapse?

1. _____

2. _____

3. _____

4. _____

5. _____

➤ What are five physical signals that you may be on the verge of slipping back into addiction or criminal behaviors?

1. _____

2. _____

3. _____

4. _____

5. _____

➤ What are five behavior signals that show you may be on the verge of slipping back into addictive behaviors?

1. _____

2. _____

3. _____

4. _____

5. _____

Behavior Chains: What Leads You to Drink or Use Other Drugs?

To prevent relapse, you need to be aware of the *behavior chains* that lead you to relapse. These chains are made up of a series of SUDs, and each one brings you a little closer to relapse.

If you can recognize your behaviors early enough, you can take action and stop the behavior chain before you do something you'll really regret—relapse.

Once you recognize your behavior chains, you can plan ways to substitute new, positive behaviors that will lead you away from relapse. In the example on page 192 about stress, talking with your partner about the stress you're feeling is a positive step in breaking the chain. Talking daily to your sponsor is another step you can take.

You need to do whatever relieves your stress before the need to drink or use is impossible to resist.

It is very important to become aware of the behaviors that will lead you to drink or use. If you can recognize them, then you can break the chain long before you get to the point of relapse. Once you recognize the links in your behavior chains, you can plan ways to substitute new, positive, and supportive behaviors to prevent relapse. You need to do whatever seems to help relieve your problems before you feel the need to turn to drugs for relief.

The next exercise can help you identify the behavior and thinking chains that lead *you* to use.

It is very important to become aware of the behaviors that will lead you to drink or use.

My Behavior Chains

➤ Look at the series of boxes on the next page. The last box of each chain contains the words *drinking or using*. Think of a time when you're likely to drink or use. Ask yourself, What was I doing just before I used? and then work backward as far as you can. Try to think of all the little steps and decisions that led up to your drinking or using. Your counselor and group members can help you do this.

FOR EXAMPLE:

Just before using, Ron was hanging out near a liquor store. He wrote that in the second to the last box. Before that, he was thinking how great it would be to have a beer again. Before that, he'd had an argument with a friend. Before that, he had been feeling depressed because he missed hanging with his old using friends. And so on.

Looking back at your answers to exercise 54 will help you do this exercise.

At this point, you might not be able to track backward more than four or five steps. Over time in recovery, you'll find that you'll become much more clear about what will lead to your drinking or using behaviors. In a month or two, come back to this exercise and add to these chains.

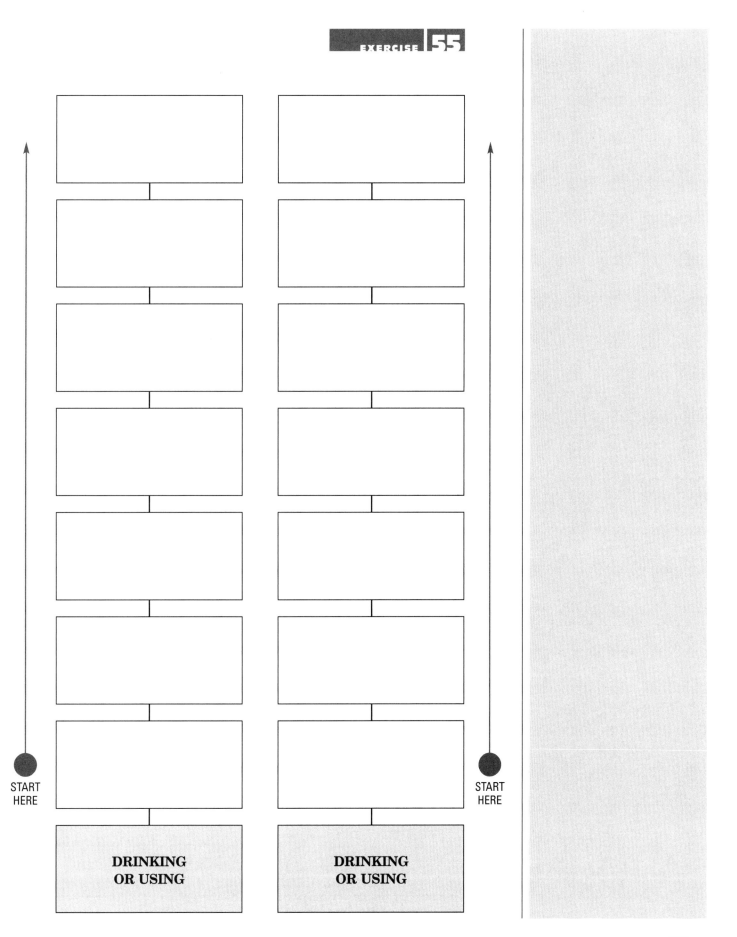

START
HERE

START
HERE

**DRINKING
OR USING**

**DRINKING
OR USING**

Intervention Cards

➤ Now that you have learned what leads to your drinking or using behaviors, you can do something about interrupting that chain by making *intervention cards*. First, you need some index cards or pieces of paper the size of index cards. Then, follow these steps:

1. On the front of one card, list the behaviors in one of the chains you completed in the previous exercise. Begin with the behavior immediately before your episode of using alcohol or other drugs.

2. On the back of the card, write some consequences that correspond to each of those behaviors.

When you're finished, each behavior on the front of your card should have a corresponding consequence on the back. If you have four behaviors, you need to have four consequences.

Here's an example:

Behaviors:	**Consequences:**
1. Going out with friends but not using.	1. Feel ashamed of myself. Start to think I could handle using.
2. Hanging out with friends who were planning to buy some crack.	2. Increase the chances I will use.
3. Talking on the phone with old friends who use.	3. Begin to lose touch with the people I need to help me stay sober.
4. Skipping support group meetings.	4. Have more time to connect with friends who continue to use.
Front	Back

➤ Next, take a second index card or piece of paper. On the front of this one, list the actions you could take to avoid drinking or using.

On the reverse side of the card, write the benefit you receive from these actions.

For example:

Behaviors:	**Benefits:**
1. Avoid hanging out with people who use or drink.	1. Avoid relapse into using or committing crimes.
2. Make friends with people who don't use and don't do criminal activities.	2. Reduce my stress, help me feel much more calm.
3. Attend support group meetings.	3. Feel positive about myself and my recovery.
4. Talk regularly with my sponsor.	4. Increase my chances of staying on the outside and not being incarcerated again.
Front	Back

When you've completed a set of cards for each behavior chain, keep them someplace where you can look at them easily. Just writing down these steps will help you remember what can lead you to relapse—and what you can do to stop the process.

When you are aware that you are in one of your drinking or using chains, pull out your cards and review them. They will remind you right away of the consequence of this behavior. They'll also give you a positive action or thought to use instead. These cards can help you make healthier choices.

If you are participating in a Twelve Step support group, you will receive a medallion marking important sobriety "birthdays," such as at three months, six months, nine months, and one year. Many people in recovery find it helpful to carry one of their medallions with them at all times to remind them of their sobriety.

Relapse Drills

Relapse drills can be another part of your relapse prevention strategy. Specific prevention skills and strategies are more helpful than vague suggestions to "stay straight."

You may think you don't need to plan, but you do. Think about professional basketball teams. They spend hours practicing set plays to use in critical situations. When there's ten seconds left in a close game, it's not the time to try some new play. They want to have the set down so they know exactly what to do.

Relapse drills serve the same purpose—except that a lot more is at stake for you! If the Lakers, Knicks, or the 76ers lose the game, they still get to come back the next game or at least the next season. If you "lose" and relapse, you're back behind bars, playing ball in the yard.

You don't want to find yourself suddenly in a potential relapse situation and have to think of what to do in the pressure of the moment.

It's better to have a solid plan

so you know exactly

what you have to do.

You may think you don't need to plan, but you do.

Relapse Drills

Certain situations are likely to trigger a relapse. Here's an example.

EXAMPLE:

You're walking home. A dealer you used to know sees you, and you stop and talk. He's got an eight-ball and asks you just to hold it for him. Choose the behaviors you need to get out of this situation without using or selling. What do you do?

➤ Describe some relapse-preventing behaviors for this example:

_____

_____

_____

_____

_____

Now think of situations that could trigger a relapse for you. (You can refer to exercise 56, Intervention Cards, to help you do these drills.) They can be while you're behind bars and after you're out. In the spaces on the next two pages, describe three situations and what you can do to prevent a relapse in each. How could you escape the "fire" without being burned? What will you say to yourself about urges and cravings? You can ask your group peers, counselor, and sponsor for help.

➤ **Potential relapse situation #1**

_____

_____

_____

Relapse-preventing behaviors:

_____

_____

_____

_____

➤ **Potential relapse situation #2**

_____

_____

_____

Relapse-preventing behaviors:

_____

_____

_____

_____

➤ **Potential relapse situation #3**

_____

_____

_____

Relapse-preventing behaviors:

_____

_____

_____

_____

 EXERCISE **58** EXERCISE

Making an Emergency Plan

Many ex-inmates carry a Sobriety Emergency Card with
them at all times. This may sound like a lame idea, but trust
us—many, many people find it _very_ helpful. It should contain

- the phone numbers of at least three people who
  are part of your sober support

- three or four easy steps you can take to get
  yourself out of a difficult situation, such as
  calling your sober support

- A few sayings or ideas that can help you in
  times when you're tempted to lapse or remind
  you why you are trying to stay sober

In the space below, write down the information you will put on your emergency card.

➤ Support people and their phone numbers:

1. _____

2. _____

3. _____

➤ Three or four easy steps you can take to get yourself out of a difficult situation

1. _____

2. _____

3. _____

4. _____

➤ Sayings or ideas that can help you:

_____

_____

_____

_____

_____

Watch for Warning Signs of the Return of Addictive or Criminal Behaviors

This is a difficult time. You are trying to make some complicated life changes. There are signals that can tell you when you are at risk for addictive or criminal behaviors. When you notice them, it's very important to get in touch with your sponsor or another person you can trust. Immediately. Here are some warning signs of addictive behaviors.

Emotional Signals

Emotional signals include being angry, stressed out, overwhelmed, anxiety stricken, lonely, sad, sorry for yourself, and bored.

Review your answers to exercises 12 and 21 where you listed why you used alcohol and other drugs and how you feel when you do. These feelings, in particular, may trigger a relapse. Being aware of when they surface can give you time to call for help.

Physical Signals

Physical signals include being tired, jumpy, irritable, impatient, restless, and excited.

Remember HALT   =   Hungry

Angry

Lonely

Tired

These four feelings can put you in a place where you're more likely to relapse. Your goal is to **AVOID** getting to the point where you're Hungry, Angry, Lonely, or Tired.

Behavioral Signals

Behavioral signals can include

- lying about your activities
- missing group or Twelve Step meetings
- missing work
- contacting old friends who still use
- being on the phone a lot to old friends who still use
- just focusing on the "outside" and not the "inside"
- working hard on changing your surroundings, not yourself
- dishonesty
- lashing out angrily at others
- fighting

Psychological Signals

Psychological signals can include thinking a lot about using, places you used to use, and so on. It may also include dangerous self-talk (what people in AA call "stinking thinking"). You use this to justify going back to drinking and using other drugs. Destructive thinking examples include

- "I can go back to my using friends."
- "I can handle drugs now that I'm better."
- "Now that I'm better, I'll just use once in a while."
- "I will use only alcohol because it was crack that got me."

Thoughts are like dominoes all stacked on end in a long line. Each domino is a thought, and each one triggers another, just like one falling domino pushes the next one, and so on. "Stinking thinking" just leads, one thought after another, to a full relapse.

"Stinking thinking" just leads, one thought after another, to a full relapse.

Psychological signals can also include the following:

- **Grandiosity:** Thinking you are more important than you are. You put yourself at the center of everything—the "big me" who has all the answers or the "poor me" who is full of self-pity.

- **Judging others:** Feeling you have the right to judge everyone else—and doing it. (AA groups call this "taking another person's inventory.)

- **Intolerance:** You want to satisfy every desire *now*. Your priorities get confused. You give more attention to passing ideas than to your real needs.

- **Impulsiveness:** You ignore the consequences of your behavior. You act without thinking.

- **Indecisiveness:** Indecisiveness and impulsiveness are close relatives. When you are impulsive, you don't consider the results of your actions. When you are indecisive, you fail to take *any* action. You exaggerate the negative things that *might* happen. Nothing gets done.

Dealing with the Stress of "Good" Feelings

Positive experiences can also be a trigger for relapse. Over the years, we have seen many addicts—both inmates and non-inmates—talk about relapses that were triggered when their lives were going well. These relapses happened when they felt a natural high and then felt an overwhelming urge to get higher—to use alcohol or other drugs. This might happen at a wedding reception, when they got a good job, after they passed their GED, or when they started a positive relationship with a partner.

You need to think about how you will deal with positive situations, too. When things are going well, it's easy to get overconfident and take your recovery for granted.

Though You're Beginning to Feel Better, Take Care!

Once you begin applying the short-term changes and start to gain control of your addiction and criminal behaviors, you will start to feel better. Probably better than you've felt in a long time.

When you start to feel better about yourself and your life, you may be tempted to stop doing this work. You may think that you've got the problem under control at last and that there's nothing more to be done. You feel strong. Confident. You might say to yourself, "I can drink or use again because, well, last time it just got a little out of control. My body is healed now, so I can handle drugs." Making this kind of change is like taking aspirin for pain. The pain may go away, but you still need to find out why it was there in the first place.

When people become overconfident in their recovery, they typically go through this cycle: they feel better, they stop working on the problem, they have another crisis, maybe a relapse, and then they start the recovery process again.

Figure 5
CONSEQUENCES OF BEING OVERCONFIDENT

BEGIN RECOVERY

FEELING BETTER

STOP WORKING ON PROBLEM

ANOTHER CRISIS OR RELAPSE

Deterrents to Addictive and Criminal Thinking Patterns

Before reading more, go back to page 124 and review these addictive patterns. Pick one thinking pattern that you often fell into. Keep focused on it when you read the following deterrents to these negative thinking patterns.

Deterrent 1:
Stop! Think of immediate consequences.

1. Before you act, think about the immediate consequences.

2. Ask, "What gets me into trouble?"

3. Think, "Smoking a joint equals incarceration."

4. Remember, if anything can go wrong, it will.

Deterrent 2:
Stop and think: Who gets hurt? Reasoning process.

1. Think about all the problems similar actions have created for you.

2. Use the bad feelings to change yourself this time.

3. Think about the whole picture or ripple effect.

Deterrent 3:
Plan ahead, think ahead, and make another choice.

1. Use this deterrent when you are reminded of exciting past actions and you want more of them. Consider the past as poison!

2. Try to predict with what person, what place, and under what circumstances you might get into trouble. Make a list ahead of time of your past thoughts and actions that equal poison.

3. Avoid troublesome people and places, and make another choice.

Deterrent 4:
Examination of conscience
(Take a daily moral inventory).

1. Think—not about the crime itself, but that *it is wrong*.

2. Think—about the injuries you have caused others.

3. Examine your conscience immediately when you start to think about irresponsible or criminal behaviors.

4. A daily moral inventory is a *preventive* tool.

Deterrent 5:
Do not dwell on it.

1. Use responsible thinking patterns to replace old patterns.

2. Before acting, use and practice responsible thinking patterns.

3. Dismiss irresponsible thoughts fast.

*"It's not just about getting out; it's about **staying** out."*

— Anonymous

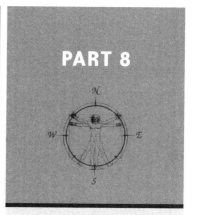

Beginning the Transition to Lifelong Change and Recovery

We call this phase of recovery the *transition.* That's because transition is the purpose of the steps you're about to take. They will help you make the change from the temporary, stop-gap measures of short-term change to the changes that support long-term recovery.

At this point in this process, people struggling with addictive behaviors often see their life in extremes or all-or-nothing terms. You might see yourself as in recovery or not in recovery—as either succeeding or failing in your efforts to deal with your compulsive or addictive behaviors.

Recovery is a process, not an event.

Recovery is a slow and steady process of change, discovery, and personal growth. Remember how the stages of change we learned about earlier overlapped at times? You can be in more than one stage at the same time. And you may sometimes have to return to previous stages before moving ahead once again. That's what the recovery process is like, too.

This stage will help you eventually make the changes that need to happen in your life for long-term recovery to take place. Right now, you'll discover that you have to do more than just manage the crisis if you want to stop drinking and using other drugs.

During this phase, it is common to feel more stress, worry, and strain. The short-term changes helped you manage your stress. Now you will begin to understand your addiction better.

It's not unusual in this stage for you to feel more depressed and worried. When this happens, it's easy to fall back into old behaviors. You might not know what to do with these feelings, so you may want to return to old habits—like using alcohol or other drugs or doing criminal activity. This reaction can become a vicious circle: (1) a crisis occurs, causing you to make some changes to control your behavior; (2) you feel better; then (3) you start to feel worse again and return to using and crime.

Miguel's Story (continued)

As I got more into recovery, I kept wanting to hurry the process. I wanted results right away, but my counselor helped me see that the results are hard to recognize at first. I realized my lack of patience was addictive thinking again: wanting what I want when I want. But even that never really happened. Once I got into crime, I was waiting a lot. Waiting for the "dope man." Waiting all day in a courtroom for a two-minute hearing. Waiting on the guards to open our cells. Waiting on chow lines, sick-call lines, and the parole board. In recovery, I learned to undo a lot of years of negative lifestyles. You can't hurry the process. It's one step at a time, one day at a time. I knew how to wait, but now, I'm waiting on something and working on something that's really worthwhile.

— Miguel, incarcerated
A New Direction program participant

Again, Watch for Denial

It's not too difficult for people who've been struggling with addiction to realize that they're in a crisis, that their behavior is out of control, and that they have to do something about it. But it's much harder to admit to a deeper and ongoing problem. This requires you to move from thinking "This is a problem" to "I have problems"—which is a much more difficult admission. It's easy to tell yourself that short-term changes will be enough in *your* situation. You might also believe that your problem isn't as bad as most people's, so *you* only need to do the short-term changes to fix it.

You might find yourself making excuses such as

- "Now that the crisis is over, I'm feeling a lot better; it must not have been that big a problem after all."

- "Other people are worse off than I am, so I don't need to do as much as they do."

- "I've been doing really well with the short-term things. I don't need to go any further. It's working."

Such attempts to minimize and justify typically happen during this stage. We'll talk about ways you can avoid or overcome such thinking. Remind yourself of just how many negative consequences you had from drinking and using other drugs.

Widening the Circle of People Who Can Help You

There are ways to make a change to a positive, happy, sober life. The following steps can help you build a new life in recovery. As you have seen, this is a lifelong journey. It's one that often requires interventions, like counseling, support groups, and spiritual guidance. It also takes time. Be patient. Remember that it took you some time to get into the situation you're in. It will likewise take some time and work for a change to take place.

We stressed earlier in this workbook how important it is to find a sponsor—a person you can trust on an ongoing basis. We hope that you have someone like that now in your life. Now, in this stage, it's time to widen the circle of people who can help you. You need to find others you can trust on an ongoing basis who know about your progress, your relapses, and what's going on with you on a regular, even daily, basis.

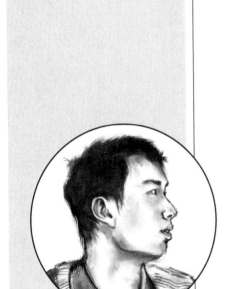

"I'm a loner who needs people."

— Anonymous

If you have access to a drug counselor now while incarcerated, talk to this person and get help. Once you have begun seeing a drug counselor, it's important to understand that there is a difference between going to counseling and actually being in counseling. "Going to counseling" means minimal involvement: showing up, sitting down, and waiting for the counselor to take charge. You don't voluntarily open up, share problems, or take any initiative. "Being in counseling" means that you come to each session with concerns and issues to work on. You have a commitment to being there mentally and emotionally, not just physically. You're there to take charge and to take responsibility for what happens. Therapy is not something your counselor "does" to you. Rather than resisting counseling, admit your need for help. Open yourself up to the struggle and pain involved in recovery rather than trying to do everything you can to avoid it.

Making Social Connections—Sober Friends

One of the keys to breaking your link with addiction and criminal behavior is simply to be with people who don't use or commit crimes. Developing positive social support is just as important and effective for your recovery as finding a helpful counselor. Your counselor can help you identify people who are incarcerated who can give you advice for making safe social connections after your release.

Involving Family and Friends

It's possible that your family was never a very positive influence on your life. Even if that's true, there's still probably someone in your family—your grandmother, an aunt or uncle—who is leading an honest, drug-free life. These family members can help you stay away from alcohol and other drugs—and from crime, too.

"Four weeks ago, a friend of mine cut his throat with a razor blade. He lived. Last night, a friend of mine hung himself in his cell. He died. Am I going to end up like them? Are you? I used to wonder about it. I even swallowed three razor blades back in 1987. I was so tired of life. I'm 35 years old and I am in prison for the fifth time. Drugs and drinking are my downfall. 100 percent. No more for me. Easy to say, but hard to do, right? AA can show us a lot if we listen. AA and treatment have given me a way out of drugs and drinking and have given me hope for the future. The more I listen, the more help I get. Like they say, 'The program works if you work it.'"

— David H.,
aggravated burglary, 20 years,
Branchville Training Center,
Indiana
(Free at Last)

Spiritual Development

Spiritual growth and development is a personal matter. Pursuing the spiritual part of yourself may involve belonging to a religious organization; following Buddhism or other spiritual traditions; doing yoga, tai chi, meditation, or relaxation exercises—to name just a few possibilities. Having someone as your spiritual guide can be very helpful. Joining a spiritual community that you can identify with is another option. Your spiritual growth can become an important part of your recovery. Many people believe that recovery can happen only with a strong spiritual foundation.

You probably have feelings of hopelessness about your addiction right now. You see that you are powerless over this disease. Your life has been out of control and unmanageable. What do you do?

You can do what literally millions of others in just this place did: They came to believe in a power outside of and greater than themselves. And they made a decision to ask for help from that higher power and from other people who understand. That power has many names: Allah, God, the Great Spirit, the Tao, Yahweh, for example.

But the name isn't important. What is important is that you believe in some power outside yourself—a power greater than yourself—that can help you overcome your addiction, that can help you stop your self-will and rely on the help of others. Maybe this sounds strange to you, but face it— you've believed in many powers greater than yourself in your old lifestyle: money, power, fame, drugs, alcohol, to name a few.

How can such a belief help you overcome addiction? Why should you believe this? These are good questions. So good, in fact, that millions of recovering people have asked them, too. Why do they believe? Because they have seen the changes in others who believed. Talk to your sponsor or your group leader or a senior peer. Ask them about this. And listen to what they say.

Addiction is a lonely illness. You became very isolated and mistrustful as an addict. It is difficult for you to believe that others will actually help you. But if you let them help, you will find the acceptance and support that will give you hope. You will realize that you don't have to do this alone. The disaster addiction and crime brought to your life comes from your being selfish. You think you know everything and are in charge of your life. But look where you are as a result—incarcerated. Nothing will change for the better as long as you keep trying to control yourself and others.

Try something different. Making a decision to ask for help from a higher power and others who understand is the step you need to take to make that change. If you stay convinced that you have all the answers, you have no chance to begin this spiritual path. Above all, you need to get rid of your selfishness. If you don't, it will kill you.

Now's the time to lead a life based on spiritual principles. To do this, you need to let go of control and take direction from a higher power and others who understand addiction.

It might seem hard to believe that something outside of you actually cares for you. Many people before you felt this way, too. But they discovered that this is true. You may not always get what you want, but you will always get what you need.

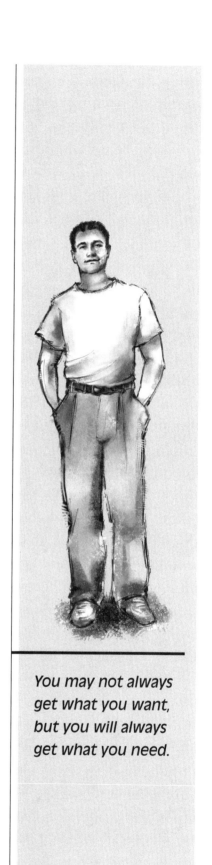

You may not always get what you want, but you will always get what you need.

Exploring the Idea of a Higher Power

➤ Draw a picture of your higher power.

➤ What do you call your higher power (name)?

_____

➤ What does your higher power call you (name)?

_____

➤ Fill in the following blanks to describe your higher power.

My higher power is . . .

_____

I am my higher power's . . .

_____

➤ My higher power is (check all that apply)

____ honest	____ unemotional
____ loving	____ compassionate
____ strong	____ playful
____ vengeful	____ understanding
____ all-knowing	____ lonely
____ just	____ overworked
____ free	____ joyful
____ apathetic	____ rigid
____ bored	____ nurturing
____ wise	____ dead
____ peaceful	____ powerless
____ perfect	____ worried
____ distant	____ resentful
____ forgiving	____ lost
____ angry	____ involved
____ sad	____ concerned
____ powerful	____ alive
____ responsible	____ punishing
____ responsive	____ gentle
____ noisy	____ stupid
____ close	____ detached
____ disappointed	____ silent

"Without a spiritual side or higher power, recovery is short-lived.... The need for a very thorough Fourth Step inventory as described in the Big Book, if done well, can almost magically remove hate, anger, and frustration by owning our part. The quality of our life is directly affected by the amount of personal responsibility we take."

— Trevor K.,
   in 16th year of life sentence
   for murder,
   Lino Lakes Correctional Facility,
   Minnesota

➤ Which statement best describes you and your higher power?

____ I am my higher power.

____ I am at one with my higher power.

____ I am a part of my higher power.

____ I am angry at my higher power.

____ I am a child of my higher power.

____ I am a servant of my higher power.

____ I am a houseguest of my higher power.

____ I am a tourist in my higher power's universe.

____ I am separated from my higher power.

____ I am divorced from my higher power.

____ I am looking for my higher power.

➤ Which roles does your higher power have in your life today? (check all that apply)

____ judge	____ mentor
____ guide/path	____ brother/sister
____ friend	____ physician/healer
____ lover	____ card partner
____ father/grandfather	____ mechanic
____ mother/grandmother	____ puppeteer
____ counselor	____ architect
____ ruler/king	____ persecutor/hit man
____ critic	____ auditor/accountant

____ battery/generator/force   ____ bartender/druggist

____ savior   ____ teacher

____ boss   ____ Santa Claus

____ police officer   ____ stranger

____ magician

➤ If you were to ask your higher power the following questions, how would your higher power answer you?

Why am I chemically dependent?

_____

_____

_____

How can I recover from my chemical dependency?

_____

_____

_____

What is the purpose of my life?

_____

_____

_____

➤ If your higher power could change you in any way, what changes would your higher power make?

_____

_____

_____

_____

_____

_____

■

Positive Values

As an addict and a criminal, you acted on the basis of your feelings. To make positive decisions, you need to develop a responsible value system and avoid acting merely on feelings.

What are values? *Values* are the beliefs a person lives by and relies on to make decisions. They are developed during childhood and act as a guide for living. As adults, we sometimes discover that some negative values we learned as a child are no longer useful. Maybe you learned, for example, that it is okay to steal to get what you want. Dishonesty is not a positive value, and it can be changed. You are not a powerless captive of your childhood environment. You do have the power to change your values.

Examples of positive values	Examples of negative values
honesty	selfishness
morality	laziness
loyalty	stealing
love of family	dishonesty
trust	violence
respect of self and others	disrespect of self and others

EXERCISE **60** EXERCISE

Positive Values

What person in your life gave you positive values to live by?

_____

_____

➤ What were those values?

_____

_____

_____

➤ When did you get away from those values?

_____

_____

_____

➤ What were your values when you were using alcohol or other drugs and committing crimes?

_____

_____

_____

➤ Do you believe it's wrong to commit a crime? Why?

_____

_____

_____

➤ With recovery comes the need for a reassessment of your values. What values do you plan to live by in your recovery?

_____

_____

_____

Miguel's Story (continued)

Now I know that living a life of recovery is much more than simply not drinking or drugging. I had to change my way of doing things. I had to change how I treated other people. I also know that life can get better—or worse—depending on how I choose to live it from this moment on. Just not using won't change your life. That's the first step, sure, but becoming the type of person who has self-respect, who's honest, and who cares for others is the real key to recovery. You can't just dry out. You've got to clean up your life, too.

I got my release six months ago. I am enrolled in some vocational technical classes and have a good job lined up. Things seem to be looking better. All I can do is take life a day at a time.

— Miguel, incarcerated
A New Direction program participant

A Final Note

Though recovery may seem to be a difficult and endless task, we encourage you to begin thinking in a new way about these changes. If you think of recovery as a burden, it won't work.

View it as an amazing opportunity. That is exactly what it is. Once you begin to change and accept the support others are offering to you, you will find that you love your new life so much that you don't want to give it up. Yes, we know that's hard to believe, but it happens. A lot.

Gradually, staying in balance will no longer seem like something you *have* to do, but something you *want* to do. You will truly begin to value what you've found. This newfound caring for yourself and the pride it creates will build a new feeling of being capable—of self-confidence, self-esteem, pride, and respect.

Even if you have not started to experience these feelings, it's important that you know that this place exists. By doing the work, you can get there. This is not a fantasy or an illusion. You can reach a point where you *want* to be in recovery. Your passion and excitement for recovery can be as strong as your passion for drinking or using and criminal activity once was.

The information, suggestions, and guidelines we've provided can start you on the road to recovery. You *can* recover. You *can* create better relationships and live a richer, more fulfilling life. Reach out to others for strength, support, and encouragement. Everything that you need will be given to you.

The Twelve Steps
of Alcoholics Anonymous

1. We admitted we were powerless over alcohol—that our lives had become unmanageable.

2. Came to believe that a Power greater than ourselves could restore us to sanity.

3. Made a decision to turn our will and our lives over to the care of God *as we understood Him.*

4. Made a searching and fearless moral inventory of ourselves.

5. Admitted to God, to ourselves, and to another human being the exact nature of our wrongs.

6. Were entirely ready to have God remove all these defects of character.

7. Humbly asked Him to remove our shortcomings.

8. Made a list of all persons we had harmed, and became willing to make amends to them all.

9. Made direct amends to such people wherever possible, except when to do so would injure them or others.

10. Continued to take personal inventory and when we were wrong promptly admitted it.

11. Sought through prayer and meditation to improve our conscious contact with God *as we understood Him,* praying only for knowledge of His will for us and the power to carry that out.

12. Having had a spiritual awakening as the result of these steps, we tried to carry this message to alcoholics, and to practice these principles in all our affairs.

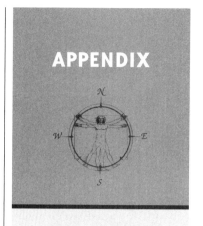

APPENDIX

A NEW DIRECTION

A Cognitive-Behavioral Treatment Curriculum

The Twelve Steps of AA are taken from *Alcoholics Anonymous,* 3d ed., published by AA World Services, Inc., New York, N.Y., 59–60. Reprinted with permission of AA World Services, Inc. (See editor's note on page 233.)

The Twelve Steps
of Narcotics Anonymous

1. We admitted we were powerless over our addiction, that our lives had become unmanageable.

2. We came to believe that a Power greater than ourselves could restore us to sanity.

3. We made a decision to turn our will and our lives over to the care of God *as we understood Him.*

4. We made a searching and fearless moral inventory of ourselves.

5. We admitted to God, to ourselves, and to another human being the exact nature of our wrongs.

6. We were entirely ready to have God remove all these defects of character.

7. We humbly asked Him to remove our shortcomings.

8. We made a list of all persons we had harmed, and became willing to make amends to them all.

9. We made direct amends to such people wherever possible, except when to do so would injure them or others.

10. We continued to take personal inventory and when we were wrong promptly admitted it.

11. We sought through prayer and meditation to improve our conscious contact with God *as we understood Him,* praying only for knowledge of His will for us and the power to carry that out.

12. Having had a spiritual awakening as a result of these steps, we tried to carry this message to addicts, and to practice these principles in all our affairs.

The Twelve-Step Alternative

1. We accept the fact that our efforts to stop using mood-altering chemicals have failed.

2. We believe that we must turn elsewhere for help.

3. We turn to our fellow men and women, particularly those who have struggled with the same problem.

4. We have made a list of the situations in which we are most likely to use mood-altering chemicals.

5. We ask our friends to help us avoid those situations.

6. We are ready to accept the help they give us.

7. We earnestly hope that they will help.

8. We have made a list of the persons we have harmed, and to whom we hope to make amends.

9. We shall do all we can to make amends, in any way that will not cause further harm.

10. We will continue to make such lists, and revise them as needed.

11. We appreciate what our friends have done, and are doing to help us.

12. We in turn are ready to help others who may come to us in the same way.

13 Feathers

Feather 1 I am a Native American. I am a Human Being. I chose not to follow the directions given by my heart of my spirit, therefore I am now chemically dependent.

Feather 2 I realize I must go back to the circle of my people, to learn the beating of our Drum and to ask the Great Spirit to restore my oneness with that circle of my people and culture, that I may one day walk once more with dignity among my people. Oh Great Spirit, hear my Drum.

Feather 3 I realize I my Drum who I am and that I must look within to find that powerful person to solve all of my problems.

Feather 4 I will search like a warrior to find my center, both fearlessly and courageously.

Feather 5 Grandfather, I stand before you. I have wronged my people, my family, and our traditions. Take pity upon me, Great Spirit.

Feather 6 Great Spirit, I come before you in a humble way. You know what is written in my heart. Help me.

Feather 7 Great Spirit, I ask you to have mercy and pity and give me the strength to fight my own greatest enemy, myself.

Feather 8 Great Spirit, I have disgraced myself and have wronged my family, my people, and our proud traditions. Oh, Great Spirit, I stand humbly before you with open arms. Great Spirit, hear me.

Feather 9 Great Spirit take pity upon me and grant me the strength that I will need to confess to my family that I have brought disgrace upon them.

Feather 10 Great Spirit Grandfather, I ask that you grant me the wisdom and the courage that I will need to keep on learning more about myself and to keep on fighting myself, that I may overcome this Chemical Dependency.

Feather 11 Oh Great Spirit, I stand in this circle of life. I am struggling here on Mother Earth. Hear my heart and grant that I may come to know myself, so that I may be a human being again among my people. Hear my heart, Grandfather.

Feather 12 I must return to our traditions, the Sacred Pipe, the sweat lodge, the drum and our people that I may once again walk among these with dignity and pride and that I may once again walk the Red Road. Hear me, Grandfather. I have found my inner arrows.

Feather 13 Before I am released from this Iron House, I will attend the Sacred Sweat Lodge and sweat my last day within this Iron House. When I come out of the Sacred Sweat Lodge, I will claim back my spirit and say, "COME, LET'S GO HOME!!!"

APPENDIX

SOS is a nonprofit network of autonomous, nonprofessional local groups dedicated solely to helping individuals achieve and maintain sobriety. There are groups meeting regularly in many cities throughout the United States.

Suggested guidelines for sobriety:

1. To break the cycle of denial and achieve sobriety, we first acknowledge that we are alcoholics or addicts.

2. We reaffirm this truth daily and accept without reservation the fact that, as clean and sober individuals, we cannot and do not drink or use, no matter what.

3. Since drinking or using is not an option for us, we take whatever steps are necessary to continue our Sobriety Priority lifelong.

4. A quality of life—"the good life"—can be achieved. However, life is also filled with uncertainties. Therefore, we do not drink or use regardless of feelings, circumstances, or conflicts.

5. We share in confidence with each other our thoughts and feelings as sober, clean individuals.

6. Sobriety is our Priority, and we are each responsible for our lives and our sobriety.

Reprinted with permission from Secular Organizations for Sobriety/Save Our Selves (SOS).

The Indian Twelve Steps
Walking the Red Road

1. We admitted we were powerless over alcohol—that we had lost control over our lives.

2. We came to believe that a Power greater than ourselves could help us regain control.

3. Made a decision to ask for help from a higher power and others who understand.

4. We stopped and thought about our strengths and our weaknesses and thought about ourselves.

5. We admitted to the Great Spirit, to ourselves, and to another person the things we thought were wrong about ourselves.

6. We are ready, with the help of the Great Spirit, to change.

7. We humbly asked a higher power and our friends to help us change.

8. We made a list of people who were hurt by our drinking and want to make up for these hurts.

9. We are making up to those people whenever we can, except when to do so would hurt them more.

10. We continue to think about our strengths and weaknesses and when we are wrong, we say so.

11. We pray and think about ourselves, praying only for strength to do what is right.

12. We try to help other alcoholics and to practice these principles in everything we do.

The Twelve Steps of Alcoholics Anonymous
Adapted for Sexual Addicts

1. We admitted we were powerless over our sexual addiction—that our lives had become unmanageable.

2. Came to believe a Power greater than ourselves could restore us to sanity.

3. Made a decision to turn our will and our lives over to the care of God, as we understood Him.

4. Made a searching and fearless moral inventory of ourselves.

5. Admitted to God, to ourselves, and to another human being the exact nature of our wrongs.

6. Were entirely ready to have God remove all these defects of character.

7. Humbly asked Him to remove our shortcomings.

8. Made a list of all persons we had harmed, and became willing to make amends to them all.

9. Made direct amends to such people wherever possible, except when to do so would injure them or others.

10. Continued to take personal inventory and when we were wrong promptly admitted it.

11. Sought through prayer and meditation to improve our conscious contact with God as we understood Him, praying only for knowledge of His will for us and the power to carry that out.

12. Having had a spiritual awakening as the result of these steps, we tried to carry this message to others and to practice these principles in all our affairs.

SMART Recovery®
Self Management and Recovery Training

SMART Recovery® is an abstinence-based, not-for-profit organization with a self-help program for people having problems with any type of addictive behavior. SMART Recovery® teaches commonsense self-help procedures designed to empower people to abstain and to develop a more positive lifestyle.

SMART Recovery®: Purposes and methods

1. We help individuals gain independence from addictive behavior.

2. We teach how to
   - enhance and maintain motivation to abstain
   - cope with urges
   - manage thoughts, feelings, and behavior
   - balance momentary and enduring satisfactions

3. Our efforts are based on scientific knowledge, and evolve as scientific knowledge evolves.

4. Individuals who have gained independence from addictive behavior are invited to stay involved with us, to enhance their gains and help others.

Reprinted with permission from SMART Recovery®

APPENDIX

The following is a list of recovery fellowships that may be helpful to you.

Adult Children of Alcoholics
(310) 534-1815
www.adultchildren.org

Alateen (ages 12–17)
(800) 356-9996
www.al-anon-alateen.org

Al-Anon
(800) 344-2666
www.al-anon-alateen.org

Alcoholics Anonymous
(212) 870-3400
www.alcoholics-anonymous.org

Co-Dependents Anonymous
(602) 277-7991
www.codependents.org

Co-Dependents of Sex Addicts
(612) 537-6904

Co-Anon
www.co-anon.org

Cocaine Anonymous
(800) 347-8998
www.ca.org

Debtors Anonymous
(781) 453-2743
www.debtorsanonymous.org

Emotions Anonymous
(651) 647-9712
www.emotionsanonymous.org

Families Anonymous
(310) 815-8010
www.familiesanonymous.org

Gamblers Anonymous
(213) 386-8789
www.gamblersanonymous.org

Marijuana Anonymous
(800) 766-6779
www.marijuana-anonymous.org

Narcotics Anonymous
(818) 773-9999
www.na.org

Nicotine Anonymous
(415) 750-0328
www.nicotine-anonymous.org

Overeaters Anonymous
(505) 891-2664
www.oa.org

Recovering Couples Anonymous
(314) 830-2600
www.recovering-couples.org

Runaway and Suicide Hotline
(800) 621-4000

S-Anon
(615) 833-3152
www.sanon.org

Sex Addicts Anonymous
(713) 869-4902
(800) 477-8191
www.sexaa.org

Sex and Love Addicts Anonymous
(781) 255-8825
www.slaafws.org

Sexual Compulsives Anonymous
(310) 859-5585
(800) 977-HEAL
www.sca-recovery.org

SMART Recovery
(440) 951-5357
www.smartrecovery.org

Survivors of Incest Anonymous
(410) 282-3400
www.siawso.org

Credits:

Free at Last: Daily Meditations by and for Inmates. Center City, Minn.: Hazelden Foundation, 1994.

Larsen, Robert E. *Chemical Dependency Handbook for Non-Medical Professionals.* Center City, Minn.: Hazelden Foundation, 1998.

Marlatt, G. Alan, and Judith R. Gordon, eds. *Relapse Prevention: Maintenance Strategies in the Treatment of Addictive Behaviors.* New York: Guilford Press, 1985.

Prochaska, James O., John C. Norcross, and Carlo C. DiClemente. *Changing for Good.* New York: Avon Books, 1995.

■   ■   ■

Editor's Note:

The Twelve Steps of Narcotics Anonymous (NA), as adapted with permission of Alcoholics Anonymous World Services, Inc. (AAWS), are reprinted with permission of Narcotics Anonymous and AAWS. The Twelve Steps of Alcoholics Anonymous are reprinted and adapted with the permission of AAWS. AAWS's permission to reprint and adapt the foregoing material does not mean that AAWS has reviewed or approved the contents of this publication, or that AAWS necessarily agrees with the views expressed herein. Alcoholics Anonymous is a program of recovery from alcoholism *only*—use or permissible adaptation of AA's Twelve Steps in connection with programs and activities which are patterned after AA, but which address other problems, or in any other non-AA context, does not imply otherwise.

APPENDIX

NOTES

_____

_____

_____

_____

_____

_____

_____

_____

_____

_____

_____

_____

_____

_____

_____

_____

_____

_____